Principles
in Practice

The Principles in Practice imprint offers teachers concrete illustrations of effective classroom practices based in NCTE research briefs and policy statements. Each book discusses the research on a specific topic, links the research to an NCTE brief or policy statement, and then demonstrates how those principles come alive in practice: by showcasing actual classroom practices that demonstrate the policies in action; by talking about research in practical, teacher-friendly language; and by offering teachers possibilities for rethinking their own practices in light of the ideas presented in the books. Books within the imprint are grouped in strands, each strand focused on a significant topic of interest.

Volumes in the Adolescent Literacy Strand

Adolescents and Digital Literacies: Learning Alongside Our Students (2010) Sara Kajder

Adolescent Literacy at Risk? The Impact of Standards (2009) Rebecca Bowers Sipe

From the Library of
Mrs. A. Villagomez

Adolescents and Digital Literacies

Learning Alongside Our Students

Sara Kajder
Virginia Tech

National Council of Teachers of English
1111 W. Kenyon Road, Urbana, Illinois 61801-1096

Staff Editor: Carol Roehm

Imprint Editor: Cathy Fleischer

Interior Design: Victoria Pohlmann

Cover Design: Pat Mayer

Cover Image: Jerry Thompson at Thompson-McClellan Photography

NCTE Stock Number: 52997

It is the policy of NCTE in its journals and other publications to provide a forum for the open discussion of ideas concerning the content and the teaching of English and the language arts. Publicity accorded to any particular point of view does not imply endorsement by the Executive Committee, the Board of Directors, or the membership at large, except in announcements of policy, where such endorsement is clearly specified.

Every effort has been made to provide current URLs and email addresses, but because of the rapidly changing nature of the Web, some sites and addresses may no longer be accessible.

Library of Congress Cataloging-in-Publication Data

Kajder, Sara B., 1975–
    Adolescents and digital literacies : learning alongside our students / Sara Kajder.
        p. cm.
    Includes biliographical references and index.
    ISBN 978-0-8141-5299-7 ((pbk) : alk. paper)
    1. Language arts (Secondary)—Computer-assisted instruction. 2. Internet in education. 3. Computer literacy. I. Title.
    LB1631.K228 2010
    428.0078'5—dc22
                                                            2009039141

Contents

Acknowledgments

This book is about teachers and students who all share the courage to believe, to take risks, to play, to re-see, and to question. You point the way for us, and it has been an honor to tell your stories. Ben Zander shared in his 2008 TED talk that "our job is to awaken possibility in others. . . . You know you're doing it when their eyes are shining." Your work, your ideas, and your practices lit my eyes and my thinking each day. More important, I know you will awaken the readers of this book.

I am incredibly grateful to the community of teachers, teacher educators, and professional colleagues who challenge my thinking and inspire new growth. Thank you to Sandy Hayes, Carl Young, Clarence Fisher, Troy Hicks, Joyce Valenza, Darren Kuropatwa, and Robyn Jackson whose words, conversations, blog posts, calls, emails, and tweets provided the right "nudge," question, connection, or support. My University of Louisville colleagues Karen Karp, Kathy Rudasill, Brenda Overturf, and Shelley Thomas helped me to find my voice and begin this work. Thank you to my VT colleagues David Hicks and Kelly Parkes, who hold me up each day and have helped me to rethink the ways in which we consider our scholarly "impact." Further, I am indebted to Dan Woods and Katie Dredger who helped me to make meaning across drafts, notes, and scribbles—and who kept our English ed program moving forward while I researched and wrote.

Thank you to my own teachers and mentors, each of whom has shared a possibility that I continually work to live into: Kylene Beers, Leila Christenbury, Robert Probst, Glen Bull, and Carol Tomlinson. Thank you to Linda Rief for the constant invitation—to learn, to visit, to laugh, to question, and to think deeply about how and why new literacy practices matter.

This work is a continuation of so many conversations with students and teachers I have taught and worked alongside at the University of Louisville and Virginia Tech, and in workshops and institutes all over the United States and Canada. Thank you for all that you do to affirm each of your students by acknowledging the multiple literacies they bring into the classroom, by creating opportunities for them to read and write in meaningful, authentic ways, and by pursuing new possibilities for what it means to teach English. You continue to teach me so much about what it means to learn together.

The National Council of Teachers of English is my professional home, and I am incredibly honored to participate in a project rooted in writing that brings together research and practice. When Cathy Fleischer shared her vision for this book and invited me to write, I was giddy both by the opportunity to share what I was seeing in the field and to work for an editor whose own work had such a significant influence on my practice and, more important, our profession. Her guidance, patience (even when my son submerged the early manuscript), insights, suggestions, and encouragement are present on each page of this book. Thank you, Cathy.

Last, I always reach to find the "right" words to thank my husband, Michael, for all that he makes possible with his support, his quiet nod while listening, and his ability to nurture our two little boys when I step away to write, to speak, to research, to teach. . . . Thank you for all you awaken in me each day.

Adolescent Literacy
An NCTE Policy Research Brief

Causes for Concern

It is easy to summon the language of crisis in discussing adolescent literacy. After all, a recent study of writing instruction reveals that 40 percent of high school seniors never or rarely write a paper of three or more pages, and although 4th and 8th graders showed some improvement in writing between 1998 and 2002, the scores of 12th graders showed no significant change. Less than half of the 2005 ACT-tested high school graduates demonstrated readiness for college-level reading, and the 2005 National Assessment of Educational Progress (NAEP) reading scores for 12th graders showed a decrease from 80 percent at the *proficient* level in 1992 to 73 percent in 2005.

Recent NAEP results also reveal a persistent achievement gap between the reading and writing scores of whites and students of color in 8th and 12th grades. Furthermore, both whites and students of color scored lower in reading in 2005 as compared with 1992, and both male and female students also scored lower in 2005.[1]

The challenges associated with adolescent literacy extend beyond secondary school to both college and elementary school. Many elementary school teachers worry about the 4th-grade slump in reading abilities. Furthermore, preliminary analysis of reading instruction in the elementary school suggests that an emphasis on processes of how to read can crowd out attention to reading for ideas, information, and concepts—the very skills adolescents need to succeed in secondary school. In the other direction, college instructors claim that students arrive in their classes ill-prepared to take up the literacy tasks of higher education, and employers lament the inadequate literacy skills of young workers. In our increasingly "flat" world, the U.S. share of the global college-educated workforce has fallen from 30 percent to 14 percent in recent decades as young workers in developing nations demonstrate employer-satisfying proficiency in literacy.[2]

In this context, many individuals and groups, including elected officials, governmental entities, foundations, and media outlets—some with little knowledge of the field—have stepped forward to shape policies that impact literacy instruction. Notably, the U.S. Congress is currently discussing new Striving Readers legislation (Bills S958 and HR2289) designed to improve the literacy skills of middle and high school students. Test scores and other numbers do not convey the full complexity of literacy even though they are effective in eliciting a feeling of crisis. Accordingly, a useful alternative would be for teachers and other informed professionals to take an interest in policy that shapes literacy instruction. This document provides research-based information to support that interest.

Common Myths about Adolescent Literacy

Myth: Literacy refers only to reading.

Reality: Literacy encompasses reading, writing, and a variety of social and intellectual practices that call upon the voice as well as the eye and hand. It also extends to new media—including nondigitized multimedia, digitized multimedia, and hypertext or hypermedia.[3]

Adolescent Literacy

Myth: Students learn everything about reading and writing in elementary school.

Reality: Some people see the processes of learning to read and write as similar to learning to ride a bicycle, as a set of skills that do not need further development once they have been achieved. Actually literacy learning is an ongoing and nonhierarchical process. Unlike math where one principle builds on another, literacy learning is recursive and requires continuing development and practice.[4]

Myth: Literacy instruction is the responsibility of English teachers alone.

Reality: Each academic content area poses its own literacy challenges in terms of vocabulary, concepts, and topics. Accordingly, adolescents in secondary school classes need explicit instruction in the literacies of each discipline as well as the actual content of the course so that they can become successful readers and writers in all subject areas.[5]

Myth: Academics are all that matter in literacy learning.

Reality: Research shows that out-of-school literacies play a very important role in literacy learning, and teachers can draw on these skills to foster learning in school. Adolescents rely on literacy in their identity development, using reading and writing to define themselves as persons. The discourses of specific disciplines and social/cultural contexts created by school classrooms shape the literacy learning of adolescents, especially when these discourses are different and conflicting.[6]

Myth: Students who struggle with one literacy will have difficulty with all literacies.

Reality: Even casual observation shows that students who struggle with reading a physics text may be excellent readers of poetry; the student who has difficulty with word problems in math may be very comfortable with historical narratives. More important, many of the literacies of adolescents are largely invisible in the classroom. Research on reading and writing beyond the classroom shows that students often have literacy skills that are not made evident in the classroom unless teachers make special efforts to include them.[7]

Myth: School writing is essentially an assessment tool that enables students to show what they have learned.

Reality: While it is true that writing is often central to assessment of what students have learned in school, it is also a means by which students learn and develop. Research shows that informal writing to learn can help increase student learning of content material, and it can even improve the summative writing in which students show what they have learned.[8]

Understanding Adolescent Literacy

Overview: Dimensions of Adolescent Literacy

In adolescence, students simultaneously begin to develop important literacy resources and experience unique literacy challenges. By fourth grade many students have learned a number of the basic processes of reading and writing; however, they still need to master literacy practices unique to different levels, disciplines, texts, and situations. As adolescents experience the shift to content-area learning, they need help from teachers to develop the confidence and skills necessary for specialized academic literacies.

Adolescents also begin to develop new literacy resources and participate in multiple discourse communities in and out of school. Frequently students' extracurricular literacy proficiencies are not valued in school. Literacy's link to community and identity means that it can be a site of resistance for adolescents. When students are not recognized for bringing valuable, multiple-literacy practices to school, they can become resistant to school-based literacy.[9]

1. Shifting Literacy Demands

The move from elementary to secondary school entails many changes including fundamental ones in the nature of literacy requirements. For adolescents, school-based literacy shifts as students engage with disciplinary content and a wide variety of difficult texts and writing tasks. Elementary school usually prepares students in the processes of reading, but many adolescents do not understand the multiple dimensions of content-based literacies. Adolescents may struggle with reading in some areas and do quite well with others. They may also be challenged to write in ways that conform to new disciplinary discourses. The proliferation of high-stakes tests can complicate the literacy learning of adolescents, particularly if test preparation takes priority over content-specific literacy instruction across the disciplines.[10]

Research says . . .

- Adolescents are less likely to struggle when subject area teachers make the reading and writing approaches in a given content area clear and visible.
- Writing prompts in which students reflect on their current understandings, questions, and learning processes help to improve content-area learning.[11]
- Effective teachers model how they access specific content-area texts.
- Learning the literacies of a given discipline can help adolescents negotiate multiple, complex discourses and recognize that texts can mean different things in different contexts.
- Efficacious teaching of cross-disciplinary literacies has a social justice dimension as well as an intellectual one.[12]

2. Multiple and Social Literacies

Adolescent literacy is social, drawing from various discourse communities in and out of school. Adolescents already have access to many different discourses including those of ethnic, online, and popular culture communities. They regularly use literacies for social and political purposes as they create meanings and participate in shaping their immediate environments.[13]

Teachers often devalue, ignore, or censor adolescents' extracurricular literacies, assuming that these literacies are morally suspect, raise controversial issues, or distract adolescents

Adolescent Literacy

from more important work. This means that some adolescents' literacy abilities remain largely invisible in the classroom.[14]

Research says . . .

- The literacies adolescents bring to school are valuable resources, but they should not be reduced to stereotypical assumptions about predictable responses from specific populations of students.
- Adolescents are successful when they understand that texts are written in social settings and for social purposes.
- Adolescents need bridges between everyday literacy practices and classroom communities, including online, non-book-based communities.
- Effective teachers understand the importance of adolescents finding enjoyable texts and don't always try to shift students to "better" books.[15]

3. Importance of Motivation

Motivation can determine whether adolescents engage with or disengage from literacy learning. If they are not engaged, adolescents with strong literacy skills may choose not to read or write. The number of students who are not engaged with or motivated by school learning grows at every grade level, reaching epidemic proportions in high school. At the secondary level, students need to build confidence to meet new literacy challenges because confident readers are more likely to be engaged. Engagement is encouraged through meaningful connections.[16]

Research says . . .

Engaged adolescents demonstrate internal motivation, self-efficacy, and a desire for mastery. Providing student choice and responsive classroom environments with connections to "real life" experiences helps adolescents build confidence and stay engaged.[17]

A. Student Choice

- Self-selection and variety engage students by enabling ownership in literacy activities.
- In adolescence, book selection options increase dramatically, and successful readers need to learn to choose texts they enjoy. If they can't identify pleasurable books, adolescents often lose interest in reading.
- Allowing student choice in writing tasks and genres can improve motivation. At the same time, writing choice must be balanced with a recognition that adolescents also need to learn the literacy practices that will support academic success.
- Choice should be meaningful. Reading materials should be appropriate and should speak to adolescents' diverse interests and varying abilities.
- Student-chosen tasks must be supported with appropriate instructional support or scaffolding.[18]

B. Responsive Classroom Environments

- Caring, responsive classroom environments enable students to take ownership of literacy activities and can counteract negative emotions that lead to lack of motivation.

- Instruction should center around learners. Active, inquiry-based activities engage reluctant academic readers and writers. Inquiry-based writing connects writing practices with real-world experiences and tasks.
- Experiences with task-mastery enable increased self-efficacy, which leads to continued engagement.
- Demystifying academic literacy helps adolescents stay engaged.
- Using technology is one way to provide learner-centered, relevant activities. For example, many students who use computers to write show more engagement and motivation and produce longer and better papers.
- Sustained experiences with diverse texts in a variety of genres that offer multiple perspectives on life experiences can enhance motivation, particularly if texts include electronic and visual media.[19]

4. Value of Multicultural Perspectives

Monocultural approaches to teaching can cause or increase the achievement gap and adolescents' disengagement with literacy. Students should see value in their own cultures and the cultures of others in their classrooms. Students who do not find representations of their own cultures in texts are likely to lose interest in school-based literacies. Similarly, they should see their home languages as having value. Those whose home language is devalued in the classroom will usually find school less engaging.

Research says . . .

Multicultural literacy is seeing, thinking, reading, writing, listening, and discussing in ways that critically confront and bridge social, cultural, and personal differences. It goes beyond a "tourist" view of cultures and encourages engagement with cultural issues in all literature, in all classrooms, and in the world.[20]

A. Multicultural Literacy across All Classrooms

- Multicultural education does not by itself foster cultural inclusiveness because it can sometimes reinforce stereotypical perceptions that need to be addressed critically.
- Multicultural literacy is not just a way of reading "ethnic" texts or discussing issues of "diversity," but rather is a holistic way of *being* that fosters social responsibility and extends well beyond English/language arts classrooms.
- Teachers need to acknowledge that we all have cultural frameworks within which we operate, and everyone—teachers and students alike—needs to consider how these frameworks can be challenged or changed to benefit all peoples.[21]
- Teacher knowledge of social science, pedagogical, and subject-matter content knowledge about diversity will foster adolescents' learning.
- Successful literacy development among English language learners depends on and fosters collaborative multicultural relationships among researchers, teachers, parents, and students.
- Integration of technology will enhance multicultural literacy.

- Confronting issues of race and ethnicity within classrooms and in the larger community will enhance student learning and engagement.[22]

B. Goals of Multicultural Literacy

- Students will view knowledge from diverse ethnic and cultural perspectives, and use knowledge to guide action that will create a humane and just world.
- Teachers will help students understand the whiteness studies principle that white is a race so they can develop a critical perspective on racial thinking by people of all skin colors.
- Multicultural literacy will serve as a means to move between cultures and communities and develop transnational understandings and collaboration.
- Ideally, students will master basic literacies *and* become mulitculturally literate citizens who foster a democratic multicultural society.[23]

Research-Based Recommendations for Effective Adolescent Literacy Instruction

For teachers . . .

Research on the practices of highly effective adolescent literacy teachers reveals a number of common qualities. Teachers who have received recognition for their classroom work, who are typically identified as outstanding by their peers and supervisors, and whose students consistently do well on high-stakes tests share a number of qualities. These qualities, in order of importance, include the following:

1. teaching with approaches that foster critical thinking, questioning, student decision-making, and independent learning;
2. addressing the diverse needs of adolescents whose literacy abilities vary considerably;
3. possessing personal characteristics such as caring about students, being creative and collaborative, and loving to read and write;
4. developing a solid knowledge about and commitment to literacy instruction;
5. using significant quality and quantity of literacy activities including hands-on, scaffolding, mini-lessons, discussions, group work, student choice, ample feedback, and multiple forms of expression;
6. participating in ongoing professional development;
7. developing quality relationships with students; and
8. managing the classroom effectively.[24]

For school programs . . .

Research on successful school programs for adolescent literacy reveals fifteen features that contribute to student achievement:

1. direct and explicit instruction;
2. effective instructional principles embedded in content;

3. motivation and self-directed learning;

4. text-based collaborative learning;

5. strategic tutoring;

6. diverse texts;

7. intensive writing;

8. technology;

9. ongoing formative assessment of students;

10. extended time for literacy;

11. long-term and continuous professional development, especially that provided by literacy coaches;

12. ongoing summative assessment of students and programs;

13. interdisciplinary teacher teams;

14. informed administrative and teacher leadership; and

15. comprehensive and coordinated literacy program.[25]

For policymakers . . .

A national survey produced action steps for policymakers interested in fostering adolescent literacy. These include:

1. align the high school curriculum with postsecondary expectations so that students are well prepared for college;

2. focus state standards on the essentials for college and work readiness;

3. shape high school courses to conform with state standards;

4. establish core course requirements for high school graduation;

5. emphasize higher-level reading skills across the high school curriculum;

6. make sure students attain the skills necessary for effective writing;

7. ensure that students learn science process and inquiry skills; and

8. monitor and share information about student progress.[26]

This report is produced by NCTE's James R. Squire Office of Policy Research, directed by Anne Ruggles Gere, with assistance from Laura Aull, Hannah Dickinson, Melinda McBee Orzulak, and Ebony Elizabeth Thomas, all students in the Joint PhD Program in English and Education at the University of Michigan.

Notes

1. ACT. (2006). *Aligning postsecondary expectations and high school practice: The gap defined: Policy implications of the ACT national curriculum survey results 2005–2006.* Iowa City, IA. Retrieved on July 3, 2007, from http://www.act.org/path/policy/pdf/NationalCurriculum Survey2006.pdf

Adolescent Literacy

Applebee, A., & Langer, J. (2006). *The state of writing instruction in America's schools: What existing data tell us*. Center on English Learning and Achievement. Retrieved on July 3, 2007, from http://cela.albany.edu

National Center for Education Statistics. (2002). *National Assessment of Educational Progress (NAEP). NAEP Writing–Average writing scale score results, grades 4, 8, and 12: 1998 and 2002*. Retrieved on July 3, 2007, from http://nces.ed.gov/nationsreportcard/writing/results2002/natscalescore.asp

National Center for Education Statistics. (2006). *National Assessment of Educational Progress (NAEP). Reading Results: Executive Summary for Grades 4 and 8*. Retrieved on July 3, 2007, from http://nces.ed.gov/nationsreportcard/reading/

2. Altwerger, B., Arya, P., Jin, L., Jordan, N. L., et al. (2004). When research and mandates collide: The challenges and dilemmas of teacher education in the era of NCLB. *English Education, 36*, 119–133.

National Center on Education and the Economy. (2007). *Tough choices or tough times: The report of the New Commission on the Skills of the American Workforce*. San Francisco, CA: Jossey-Bass.

3. Brandt, D. (2001). *Literacy in American lives*. New York: Cambridge University Press.

Gee, J. (2007). *Social linguistics and literacies: Ideology in discourses*. London: Taylor & Francis.

4. Franzak, J. K. (2006). *Zoom*. A review of the literature on marginalized adolescent readers, literacy theory, and policy implications. *Review of Educational Research, 76*, 2, 209–248.

5. Sturtevant, E., & Linek, W. (2003). The instructional beliefs and decisions of middle and secondary teachers who successfully blend literacy and content. *Reading Research & Instruction, 43*, 74–90.

6. Guzzetti, B., & Gamboa, M. (2004). 'Zines for social justice: Adolescent girls writing on their own. *Reading Research Quarterly, 39*, 408–437.

Langer, J. (2001). Beating the odds: Teaching middle and high school students to read and write well. *American Educational Research Journal, 38*, 4, 837–880.

Nielsen, L. (2006). Playing for real: Texts and the performance of identity. In D. Alvermann, K. Hinchman, D. Moore, S. Phelps, & D. Waff (Eds.), *Reconceptualizing the literacies in adolescents' lives* (2nd ed.) Mahwah, NJ: Lawrence Erlbaum, 5–28.

Sturtevant, E. & Linek, W. (2003).

7. Moje, E. B. (2002). Re-framing adolescent literacy research for new times: Studying youth as a resource. *Reading Research and Instruction, 41*, 211–228.

8. Boscolo, P., & Mason, L. (2001). Writing to learn, writing to transfer. In G. Jijlaarsdam, P. Tynjala, L. Mason, & K. Londa (Eds.), *Studies in writing: Vol 7. Writing as a learning tool: Integrating theory and practice*. Dordrecht, The Netherlands: Kluwer Academic Publishers, 83–104.

9. Lenters, K. (2006). Resistance, struggle, and the adolescent reader. *Journal of Adolescent and Adult Literacy, 50*(2), 136–142.

10. Moje, E. B., & Sutherland, L. M. (2003). The future of middle school literacy education. *English Education, 35*(2), 149–164.

Snow, C. E., & Biancarosa, G. (2003). *Adolescent literacy and the achievement: What do we know and where do we go from here?* New York: Carnegie Corporation. Retrieved June 23, 2007, from http://www.all4ed.org/resources/CarnegieAdolescentLiteracyReport.pdf

11. Bangert-Drowns, R. L., Hurley, M. M., & Wilkinson, B. (2004). The effects of school-based writing-to-learn interventions on academic achievement: A meta-analysis. *Review of Educational Research, 74*, 29–58.

Greenleaf, C. L., Schoenbach, R., Cziko, C., & Mueller, F. (2001). Apprenticing adolescent readers to academic literacy. *Harvard Education Review, 71*(1), 79–129.

12. Moje, E. B., Ciechanowski, K. M, Kramer, K., Ellis, L., Carrillo, R., & Collazo, T. (2004). Working toward third space in content area literacy: An examination of everyday funds of knowledge and discourse. *Reading Research Quarterly, 39*(1), 38–70.

13. Moje, E. B. (2007). Developing socially just subject-matter instruction: A review of the literature on disciplinary literacy. N. L. Parker (Ed.), *Review of research in education.* (pp. 1–44). Washington, DC: American Educational Research Association.

14. Kim, J. L. W., & Monique, L. (2004). Pleasure reading: Associations between young women's sexual attitudes and their reading of contemporary women's magazines. *Psychology of Women Quarterly, 28*(1), 48–58.

Kliewer, C., Biklen, D., & Kasa-Hendrickson, C. (2006). Who may be literate? Disability and resistance to the cultural denial of competence. *American Educational Research Journal, 43*(2), 163–192.

Moje, E. B., & Sutherland, L. M. (2003).

15. Moje, E. B. (2007).

Ross, C. S. (2001). Making choices: What readers say about choosing books for pleasure. In W. Katz (Ed.), *Reading, Books, and Librarians.* New York: Haworth Information Press.

16. Guthrie, J. T., Van Meter, P., McCann, A. D., Wigfield, A., Bennett, L., & Poundstone, C. C. (1996). Growth of literacy engagement: Changes in motivations and strategies during concept-oriented reading instruction. *Reading Research Quarterly, 31*, 306–332.

17. Guthrie, J. T. (2001). Contexts for engagement and motivation in reading. *Reading Online.* International Reading Association. Retrieved June 23, 2007, from http://www.readingonline.org/articles/handbook/guthrie/index.html

Guthrie, J. T., & Humenick, N. M. (2004). Motivating students to read: Evidence for classroom practices that increase reading motivation and achievement. In P. McCardle and V. Chhabra (Eds.), *The voice of evidence in reading research.* Baltimore, MD: Brookes, 329–54.

Adolescent Literacy

18. Biancarosa, G., & Snow, C. (2004). *Reading next: A vision for action and research in middle and high school literacy. Report to Carnegie Corporation of New York.* Washington, DC: Alliance for Excellent Education. Retrieved June 25, 2007, from http://www.all4ed.org/publications/ReadingNext/ReadingNext.pdf

Guthrie, J. T. (2001).

Oldfather, P. (1994). *When students do not feel motivated for literacy learning: How a responsive classroom culture helps.* College Park, MD: University of Maryland, National Reading Research Center. Retrieved June 25, 2007, from http://curry.edschool.virginia.edu/go/clic/nrrc/rspon_r8.html; NCREL (2005).

19. Goldberg, A., Russell, M., & Cook, A. (2003). The effects of computers on student writing: A meta-analysis of studies from 1992 to 2002. *Journal of Technology, Learning, and Assessment, 2*, 1–51.

Greenleaf et al. (2001).

Guthrie, J. T. (2001).

Kamil, M. (2003).

Ray, K. W. (2006). Exploring inquiry as a teaching stance in the writing workshop. *Language Arts, 83*(3), 238–248.

20. Hade, D. (1997). Reading multiculturally. In V. Harris (Ed.), *Using multiethnic literature in the K-8 classroom.* Norwood: Christopher-Gordon.

Cai, M. (1998). Multiple definitions of multicultural literature: Is the debate really just "ivory tower" bickering? *New Advocate, 11*, 4, 11–24.

Taxel, J. (1992). The politics of children's literature: Reflections on multiculturalism, political correctness, and Christopher Columbus. In V. Harris (Ed.), *Teaching multicultural literature in grades K-8.* Norwood: Christopher-Gordon.

21. Fang, Z., Fu, D., & Lamme, L. (1999). Rethinking the role of multicultural literature in literacy instruction: Problems, paradox, and possibilities. *New Advocate, 12*(3), 259–276.

Nieto, S. (2000). *Affirming diversity: The sociopolitical context of multicultural education.* New York: Longman.

Rochman, H. (1993). Beyond political correctness. In D. Fox & K. Short (Eds.), *Stories matter: The complexity of cultural authenticity in children's literature.* Urbana: NCTE.

Taxel, J. (1992).

22. Banks, J. A. (1991). Teaching multicultural literacy to teachers. *Teaching Education, 4*, 1, 135–144.

Feuerverger, G. (1994). A multicultural literacy intervention for minority language students. *Language and Education, 8*, 3, 123–146.

Diamond, B. J., & Moore, M. A. (1995). Multicultural literacy: Mirroring the reality of the classroom. New York: Longman.

Freedman, S. W. (1999). *Inside city schools: Investigating literacy in multicultural classrooms.* New York: Teachers College Press.

23. Banks, J. A. (2004). *Handbook of research on multicultural education*. San Francisco: Jossey-Bass.

Jay, G. S. (2005). Whiteness studies and the multicultural literature classroom. *MELUS, 30*(2), 99-121.

Luke, A., & Carpenter, M. (2003). Literacy education for a new ethics of global community. *Language Arts, 81*(1), 20.

24. Applebee, A., Langer, J., Nystrand, M., & Gamoran, A. (2003). Discussion-based approaches to developing understanding: Classroom instruction and student performance in middle and high school English. *American Educational Research Journal, 40*, 685–730.

Paris, S. R., & Block, C. C. (2007). The expertise of adolescent literacy teachers. *Journal of Adolescent & Adult Literacy, 50*, 7, 582–596.

25. Biancarosa, G., & Snow C. E. (2004).

26. ACT, 2006.

This publication of the James R. Squire Office of Policy Research offers updates on research with implications for policy decisions that affect teaching and learning. Each issue addresses a different topic. Download this issue at http://www.ncte.org/library/NCTEFiles/Resources/Positions/chron0907ResearchBrief.pdf.

Chapter One

Situating the Conversation: New Literacies, Technology, and Learning in the English Language Arts Classroom

Meet Jassar.[1] He is a student in fifth period, tenth-grade English. At the start of the semester, his name appeared on the initial class roster coated in yellow highlighter and annotated with words he carried like baggage from the previous term—*non-reader, below-level, at-risk*. He sits in the right rear corner of the classroom, behind more vocal and active students who provide a bit of a shield from the teacher's questions and eyes. Assessments tell us that he is reading on a sixth-grade level (but it has been a year since he's been willing to fill out a Scantron sheet), and he struggles to write by hand. By all of the measures that we use in school, Jassar is underperforming and lacking in literacy skills.

And outside of school? Jassar is active in service learning, organizing and leading projects for middle and high school youth through his church. To anchor this work, he has developed an annotated Google Map of the community, placing a "pin" and a written description noting the site, work, and participants in a specific project. So, cursoring over the community center will reveal a description of a project completed in September in which three high school students built a new walkway to support handicapped access to the building, and cursoring over the high school will reveal the ongoing hours for the student-run food bank. Some of the annotations include images of students and community members working together at the corresponding site. The site is open for community access and is "publicized" by flyers Jassar has posted in high-traffic areas (like the teen rec center, the community library, and the local post office) and distributed for peers to hand out within the town. To share the link with digital youth, he has created a Facebook group and a page on MySpace, and is beginning to develop a Ning to support collaboration and community among those who have worked on local community projects. Fueled by his interests in community service, Jassar is now working to build/design a group for American teens that accomplishes the same goals/outcomes as kiva.org, a website which helps to support the work of international entrepreneurs who are working to lift themselves out of poverty.

Across all of his work, Jassar has demonstrated a broad range of literacy practices, none of which he was "taught" inside of school. He has leveraged specific media (e.g., Google My Maps) to create a multimodal resource using both print text and image to organize and archive the work of a community in providing service in a variety of ways and contexts. He has identified the dominant media forms for target populations (e.g., the Ning for digital youth and print flyers for non-digital community members) and communicated both a need for action and organized plans in support of a set goal. As a self-directed learner, he has researched the needs and contexts of individuals within his own community and abroad in an attempt to better position his own work. And he has collaborated with and mobilized peers and adult community members.

Jassar is vibrantly literate in ways that are purposeful and important, and in ways that have a place in a classroom that values bringing together his digital literacy skills; his passion for doing work that "matters" outside of school walls; his need to interact with expert, authentic audiences; *and* the diverse texts, skills, and experiences that make up our English curricula. This book is about the work of imagining and building the English classroom where Jassar (and his peers) might come alive as engaged readers and writers. It is meant to invite critical discussion around what it means to teach and learn in a digital age steeped in social media while raising ideas about how we leverage that media to foster reading and writing. And, most important, it is about capturing the stories of teachers and students (like

[handwritten margin note: Be careful to not disregard relevant literacies — should not be a school outside disconnect]

Jassar) who are working to bring new literacy practices into the English classroom in ways that are authentic and meaningful, and that invite (and incite) real participation and learning.

Teaching in a "New" English Classroom

This is an exhilarating (and genuinely daunting) time to teach English. We are in the midst of significant changes in how we read and write and where we learn to do either. And it is all happening rapidly. Beginning with Guttenberg's time, change happened over the course of centuries, whereas the very real and significant changes in literate practice that mark our time have unfolded over only the past few decades. And the rate of change is on the increase.

Excitement and challenge ever-changing drastic

A handful of words and phrases used throughout our professional discourse and literature capture these changes. We read about new literacies, twenty-first-century literacies, and multimodal literacies, all of which are to lead our work with adolescents who are described as millennials, Generation Y, the 'Net Generation, digital natives, and the MEdia Generation. They have come of age during a time marked by social media and tools that have emerged from what is simultaneously and interchangeably called Web 2.0 and the read-write Web. And when we listen to our students (and our "plugged-in" colleagues), we hear about technologies that allow us to tweet, stream, remix, text, friend, and geocache.

This book is less about "translating" these new technology terms (which will be outdated and obsolete before this book appears in print) and more about how we work as English teachers to navigate a changing landscape—and how we lead our students to do the same. This is work that is about openings, creativity, ingenuity, and rethinking our practice. But it is also about proceeding in intentional and deliberate ways. Early into my teaching, as I worked within a "new" computer lab outfitted with fifteen Apple Classic IIe machines (ten of which worked at any given moment and two of which could be on the dial-up network at a time), my thinking was focused on what I could make a tool do. Now, sitting in classrooms where a single student's cell phone has more computing power than I had in that early computer lab, my approach has changed to focusing on what I *want* the tool to do. It is a small shift in thinking, but one that has big implications for my teaching. It isn't about the tools. It is about reading, writing, communicating, and pedagogy.

focus, what is important

The kids (and, in some cases, teachers) with whom I work talk daily about their digital lives and online practices in a language that doesn't sound like anything that appears in my curricular guides or state standards. They play and communicate with different text forms, modes, and media from the traditional content in our curricula and practices. And that is a good thing. I want my students reading and writing, communicating and publishing. The energy and excitement that come from teaching English now are rooted in the same "core" that I've always valued—the opportunity and privilege to help kids work as intentional, self-directed, reflective learners who are able to make meaning from and with a range of texts and then share their knowledge and understandings in smart and meaning-ful ways. But our work now is about a broader English curriculum, one leveraging the unique practices students bring to the classroom as readers, writers, viewers, and users of a variety of textual spaces (digital and print) in order to teach both traditional practices of reading and writing *and* new literacy practices ranging from information literacy to working in online communities to composing with a variety of media.

And I can't make that shift alone. As much as I work to co-construct literacy practices alongside students, whether they are adolescents or graduate students, I also turn to my professional communities for support, insights, and a push to continue to rethink my practice and continue to really see kids. My most important professional learning has always come from my experiences with NCTE, whether reading my colleagues' work in our journals, engaging in the unique spaces pro-vided at our conventions, or now reading and thinking critically about *Adolescent Literacy: An NCTE Policy Research Brief.*

"Unpacking" Adolescent Literacy: An NCTE Policy Research Brief

Documents like this often come across our desks or inboxes, offering a summary or synthesis of research and policy recommendations but, for me, rarely impacting much of what I do with my students. That said, *Adolescent Literacy: An NCTE Policy Research Brief* (AL Brief) is different in that it was written with the goal of pulling together what we know about adolescent literacy right now in an attempt to do something better with and for our students. It came at just the right time as I was thinking deeply about my practice, trying to find new ways to engage and motivate the adolescents in the classrooms in which I work, and seeking a text that could help to move teachers' practice.[2]

I asked specific things of the AL Brief, first looking at it through the lens of a teacher and teacher educator working to better understand students; the ways in which they work with and address the dominant media of their time; and the inter-sections with the English curricula, great books, and practices that I value. I read it also through the lens of a teacher educator and researcher who is seeing changes as she participates in secondary classrooms (seeing literature circle groups that bring in participants through webcams or classes of students that mark up pieces of writing using a smart board), but who wants to know more about the impact of those changes on student learning. I read in a way that is similar to how I approach research and pedagogical articles, using the findings and ideas captured in the brief as a lens through which my students and classroom might appear different, strange, and new. I used it as a tool, a frame, and a text challenging me to push back. It is that "push back" that I aim to capture in this book as I offer a look at students, learning contexts, pedagogy, and literacy practices in an attempt to better understand where we are and where we need to go next.

So, how does this document work? Starting by establishing need and context (i.e., sharing data that establishes that students' scores on literacy assessments are far from what we want to see and that students' success after graduation hinges on skills that, at this point in time, few demonstrate), the document moves into a discussion aimed at debunking many of the things I often hear when talking with colleagues: that "academics are all that matter in literacy learning" or that "students learn everything about reading and writing in elementary school." As much as I see the realities playing out daily in the schools in which I work, seeing them described here in print challenges me to think about practice differently. I read the realities as almost reminders, as these are challenging ideas that force me to not only tweak a lesson or two but also rethink the bigger structure of and vision within my teaching. It is easy to nod in agreement when I read a myth statement like, "Students who struggle with one literacy will have difficulty with all literacies." Sure, I know that myth to be false because I see what my students bring to their classroom work. Still, it is much more difficult to make changes in my pedagogy that affirm the ways in which my students come multiply literate and to build scaffolds and instructional tasks that will leverage and build on those literacies. More simply put, using what is said in the "reality" descriptions to inform and guide my teaching is important, yet it is difficult, often messy work.

Immediately following the section on the myths and realities of adolescent literacy, the document focuses on establishing what we know by situating what is changing/different/necessary for us to know in the emerging research. I use this kind of research in two ways: one, to give me a sense of the "substance" behind a new idea or instructional strategy (as I need to see a compelling argument and set of results in order to invest the time needed to build something new into my teaching); and, two, to provide me with "backup" that helps me to explain our work in the classroom to parents or administrators who can sometimes become skittish when an English classroom looks different from what they might expect.

A case in point: At the onset of the semester, I worked with a classroom teacher to "re-invent" a writing activity from one that simply asked students to write a short memoir to a task in which they were asked to compose and produce a two- to three-minute digital story that paired images, narration (of a written script), and motion to create a filmic version of that same piece of writing. And, using ustream.tv, we were scheduled to stream/share these with students in three other classrooms in the district for their feedback and input as peers and peer reviewers. To do this meant that the students in this class needed access to a computer lab—which also meant that the beginning of the semester setup that was to be run on our cart of laptops had to happen quickly. To move the chain of events, we needed some backup, and so we turned to the AL Brief (all page numbers cited are from the Web version) to help us summarize and present pertinent research to administration (and our tech-support folks), arguing:

1. Adolescents need bridges between everyday literacy practices and classroom communities (3).

2. Caring, responsive classroom environments enable students to take ownership of literacy activities and can counteract negative emotions that lead to lack of motivation (4).

3. Using technology is one way to provide learner-centered, relevant activities. For example, many students who use computers to write show more engagement and motivation and produce longer and better papers (4).

I read the AL Brief in my current role as a teacher educator and researcher working alongside students and teachers in diverse contexts across the United States, and as a former middle and high school English teacher. More important, I come to the brief as a learner working alongside my students to navigate our increasingly digital world. In the pages to come, I both model how I've operationalized the recommendations and ideas in the brief and share some of the additional theory and research that inform my work in each of these roles. In doing so, I explore samples of student work, descriptive cases of classroom work and contexts, and instances of "teacher talk" as think-alouds presenting the kinds of moves that we make in planning, executing, and reflecting on instruction that supports the kinds of new literacies learning that the brief recommends.

Reseeing Jassar's Story

Let me begin this work by looking again at Jassar's experiences, this time through the lens provided by the AL Brief. Reading across the many significant ideas raised in the brief, I began to generate my own list of "big ideas." Several of these are now listed on the inside of my lesson planner, as I need regular reminders to think beyond the classroom as I was trained to see it:

1. **Kids come to us multiply literate.**
   At the start of the document, and throughout each section, we are reminded that literacy "encompasses reading, writing, and a variety of social and intellectual practices that call upon the voice as well as the eye and the hand . . . including nondigitalized multimedia, digitized multimedia, and hypertext or hypermedia" (2). Jassar's literacy certainly

demonstrates this expanded notion of the reading and writing practices in which many teens are engaged—as he creates a variety of genres from pages on social networking sites to flyers. And what is equally clear from Jassar's story is this: "Many of the literacies of adolescents are largely invisible in the classroom" (2). When I think of what this means for us as English teachers, I recognize we must continually work with multiple texts, modes, and media in an attempt to make meaning and communicate understanding.

2. **Literacy is social, active, and connective.**
Adolescents are, by nature, social. And they use "literacies for social and political purposes as they create meanings and participate in shaping their immediate environments," much as Jassar did in his mapping project (3). As an English teacher, this idea pushes me to continue to seek ways to create "bridges between everyday literacy practices and classroom communities" and to help students understand that "texts are written in social settings for social purposes," something Jassar intuitively understands already (3). Connectiveness is about participation and fostering community inside both the classroom and the greater network in which we can work (i.e., alongside experts, peers, colleagues, community members).

3. **Kids need to be able to answer "We are doing this in order to . . . "**
When kids are engaged, as Jassar was in his project, they "demonstrate internal motivation, self-efficacy, and a desire for mastery" (3). The question for us as teachers becomes this: how do we turn our classrooms into sites where the kind of engagement and motivation Jassar exhibits becomes the norm, that grows from a smart, intentional melding of student choice, teacher-constructed instructional scaffolds leading to success, and inquiry-based, real-world experiences for authentic audiences (3)? As we'll see in the work ahead, technology is just one piece of this; the core is about much bigger ideas (including but not limited to creativity, originality, critical thinking, diverse perspectives, and sustained experiences).

Reseeing the Classroom through Theory and Research

In thinking about how new or multiple literacies would have meaning in my classroom work, my natural first step was to think about my own definition of literacy and how it has changed and developed over the years. As a young secondary school teacher, I started where many of us likely did, seeing reading and writing as print-centric. It wasn't until I spent time in complex, richly diverse classrooms that I started to push against that definition, looking for ways to affirm the many skill sets that students brought into the classroom that provided unique affordances for constructing and communicating meaning, but not always in ways that fit easily into school contexts.

The dissonance that emerged as I thought deeply about what I believed about literacy was the most heightened during activities and projects in which students were using technology—writing digital stories, completing WebQuests, or collaborating with other students (and experts) in online communities. In the early work I did with students using iMovie or Photoshop, the roles of reader and writer seemed blurred, as were those between producer and consumer. Technology provided us (teacher and students) with new opportunities, new tools, new communities—and a complex range of skills, knowledge, and understandings that were ever-developing as the tool set continued to change at an unprecedented rate. But was it the technology that led to these changes or was it a changing understanding of literacy itself? The more I read and the more I thought about what was happening in our classroom, the more I became convinced that the changing motivation and participation I was seeing was less about the specific technologies and more about new ways of thinking about students' literacies and learning.

As I begin to unpack this, it helps me to think about the some of the terms we use to describe the new kinds of learning that are going on in twenty-first-century classrooms. What difference does it make, for example, when we shift our language from *literacy* to *literacies*—a shift made even murkier by the multiple terms we use to describe this phenomenon? We talk about *multiple literacies*, *multimodality*, *twenty-first-century literacies*, *out-of-school literacy*, *digital literacy*, and *new literacies* in what is almost the same breath. As I have grown as a teacher and researcher, I found I've needed to get a sense of how these terms all worked individually and together in order to make sense out of how they could play into and inform my teaching.

We live in a digital age in which the tools (and the literacies they require and, at times, create) change almost overnight. As Mahiri (2006) argues, "Traditional conceptions of print-based literacy do not apprehend the richness and complexity of actual literacy practices in people's lives enabled by new technologies that both magnify and simplify access to and creation of multimodal texts" (61). Thinking in terms of multiple literacies allows me to work with multiple communication modes (e.g., linguistic, visual, oral, audio, and kinesthetic) in constructing and communicating intended meaning (Cope and Kalantzis 4). Adding digital literacies to the mix challenges me to examine practices tied to constructing and critically understanding the modes made possible by digital tools.

A further level of important difference comes when we draw out the distinctions between new literacies and multimodality. Researchers, teachers, and students who focus on new literacy studies (New London Group 62) examine people in interaction with one another and what they are doing with texts. Those who focus on multimodalities (Kress and Street vii) study what we understand about the tools that people are using in intentional ways and purposeful contexts. Looking at our English classrooms through a new literacies lens challenges us to think about the modes through which students are making meaning (inside and outside of our classrooms) and the ways that students do (or don't) use appropriate, well-chosen modes to communicate their understanding.

The distinction between these two lenses is important, because it suggests that our thinking about multiple literacies doesn't *have* to require talk about digital technologies. The notion of *literacies* (and all that this term implies) is not dependent on digital knowledge or prowess. However, I (and many others) have found it useful to consider the place of digital technologies and multimodalities within the concept of multiple literacies—especially as we think about the skills and practices students now need to be successful readers and writers outside our classrooms and the practices that, once denied, have led them to become increasingly resistant to a classroom that valued and provided opportunities only for exercising print-based literacy. For students in my class to be literate, in other words, they needed to know how to make meaning from different text forms and communication modes and how to communicate through those modes. They needed to know how to use those media to learn, inform, investigate, reveal, advocate, and organize (Rheingold 109). This was a big change, and not one readily found in my curriculum guides.

Like many teachers, my increasing understanding of multiple literacies has been even more complicated by the timing of the research that supported it, coinciding with (and often shelved by) another new set of terms: *NCLB, AYP,* and *high-stakes testing.* So as texts and tool sets outside of our classrooms have become increasingly diverse and complex, curriculum and assessments written and disseminated during this time have narrowed our view of literacy. Perhaps that is part of the reason that I find the AL Brief to be so important. Though I have worked throughout my teaching to provide students with rich opportunities to exercise and engage in the literacies that they need to be productive participants in our communities inside and outside of our classrooms, it is compelling that we have a document that brings together the research in adolescent literacy in a way that says you aren't alone in what you are seeing, what you are doing is in line with what research tells us, and, most important, here is what you do next as new literacies continue to emerge. And it is vital to have such a document in a time of increasingly mandated curriculum and high-stakes testing, as a reminder and a touchstone for ways of teaching and learning that support flexibility, creativity, invention, and facilitation.

There are qualities to the latest rush of new media and new technologies (i.e., Web 2.0) that make them of particular interest to the English classroom. The new media and tools that mark Web 2.0 are often described as *participatory* tools in that they position the user to create, to interact, to publish, and to share with audiences, groups, and other social environments available online. It is the social nature of this

Web 2.0 social impact

work that sets it apart from other digital advances as "participatory media shape the cognitive and social environments in which twenty-first-century life will take place in much the same way that print culture shaped the environment in which the Enlightenment blossomed" (Rheingold 98). Thus, students who are literate in Web 2.0 tools (e.g., podcasting, participating in wikis, blogging) are positioned to create and publish knowledge through multiple modalities and, in many cases, collective action. Or, to use the language from the brief, "Adolescents regularly use literacies for social and political purposes as they create meanings and participate in their immediate environments" (3).

need for shift/ "opening up"

In this work, it is important to understand that valuing multiple literacies and finding ways for students to exercise them in the classroom is not a move to threaten or "replace" the print-based work that remains at the core of our formal curricula. One does not replace the other (Mahiri 7; Moje et al., "Teenagers"). Instead, I see this shift as an opportunity to open up what "counts" as valued communication, to invite voices into our classroom that would formerly not be present, and to help students in practicing (and critically unpacking) the dominant modes and media of their time. Adolescents are increasingly finding their own reasons to become literate, especially when learning a literate practice allows them to collaborate with and participate within a group that values their knowledge/contribution (Gee 105; NCTE). When we as teachers open ourselves up to learn about those literacy practices, the ways in which motivation and engagement play into the work, and the communities that develop, we can begin to imagine new ways for extending and elaborating on the literacies students bring into our classrooms, again bridging between the world outside of the classroom and the world we are looking to build.

Looking into Our Practice

New literacies, new technologies, new ways of reading and writing . . . In real ways, these are invitations to rethink and reimagine our work as English teachers, as readers, as writers, and as individuals who have our own literacy identities. In the pages that follow, I work to use the ideas, research, and recommendations articulated in the AL Brief as a framework around which to explore classroom practices, student work, and teacher thinking when it comes to teaching with digital tools and multimodal practices in twenty-first-century secondary English classrooms. The goal won't be to teach you where to point and click when implementing a particular strategy or tool, but to discuss critically the ways that new tools impact our pedagogy, create new roles for teachers and students, and establish new pressures on and opportunities for our curricula and assessment tools. I will talk about the role of creativity and community in our classrooms; about collaborative inquiry, participation, and what it means to learn with our students; and about how we lead students to be serious students of literature and language while also fostering the multiple literacies made possible in and even required by our increasingly participatory culture.

We can learn from looking closely at our practice, the practice of our colleagues, and the ways that our students move and learn both in and outside of our classrooms. To that end, I work throughout the book to bring together examples from multiple classrooms across the United States in which I've worked as a researcher, a "coach," a coordinator of student teachers, and a teacher educator. In doing so, I hope to present such a varied (and yet rich) range of examples and voices that you'll see your classrooms here, that you'll hear an echo of a student whom you know, and that you'll see possibility in what a colleague with a shared perspective or context was able to move forward. I also hope to be transparent about practice and learning because, for all of us, this is new work, and it requires conversations about change, about struggle, about triumph, and about the days where the power went out.

And the goal? Thinking back to Jassar's experiences, I can't help but set my measure for success at whether I am able to mindfully and purposefully engage his work as a reader and a writer within our English classroom. I've said that this work is less about the technology and more about the pedagogy. But the most important piece for me is in our students.

In this book, we'll look into real classrooms with real kids. Some classrooms have little more than one computer and few kids have consistent access at home. It is messy work. So, while these aren't examples offering an "easy button," they are examples that will give you access to kids' voices and a glimpse into what is possible when we bring together the literacies they bring to the classroom and the unique knowledge and goals that we have as English teachers. Our students need us to provide them with rich opportunities to read deeply, think critically, and write for responsive audiences. And they need us to prepare them for a world outside of our classrooms where literacy, texts, and tools will continue to change, be recast, and even reinvent themselves. When I spoke with him about school, literacy, and what was and wasn't working for him, Jassar shared that "the technology is invisible to me, except when I come into school. It's like you all haven't figured out that I'm digital now. I get that [technology] isn't invisible to you—but how can this place be about learning if it plays like what I see doesn't even exist?" This book is about ways that we work alongside Jassar to construct an English classroom that engages him through multiple modes, media, and literacies as a reader and writer; sets the bar high; and puts his knowledge to work in relevant, authentic, and challenging ways.

Notes

1. Pseudonyms are used throughout this book for student names, teacher names, and school names.

2. A quick note about the various roles I occupy: I am a former secondary school English teacher, now a college professor of English education. In this second role, I have the opportunity to teach graduate and undergraduate students, supervise student teachers, and constantly visit classes.

Digital Youth

 Technology is only technology for people who are born before it was invented.

—Alan Kay (qtd. in Dan Tapscott *Grown Up Digital*)

[Digital youth] can be **"always on,"** in constant contact with friends via texting, instant messaging, mobile phones, and Internet connections. . . .

—*Living and Learning with New Media Report*, 2008

Growing Up in a Digital Age

Walking down the crowded hallways of a high school can often be a challenging feat—dodging students, avoiding the unknowing "swing" of a loaded backpack from a student's shoulder, all while attempting to get to a specific destination in a finite amount of time. Today, that journey didn't go well. Instead of skillfully weaving my way down to the library, I got stuck within a slow-moving stream of students and, as I'm not quite 5 feet tall, looking outside of the stream for an exit wasn't a realistic option.

I merged alongside Doug, a tenth-grade student who was known to teachers and peers as a smart, engaged thinker. We'd met when I'd recently observed a student teacher in his English class, and bit my tongue (painfully) while watching him type on his cell phone from behind a stack of books on his desk. Today, as I would again see him during a third-period observation, I nodded a hello and caught his eyes on the book I held on top of a pile of notebooks (a copy of *Born Digital*, a study by scholars at Harvard examining the daily practices of "digital youth" [Palfrey and Gasser]). He asked if I was reading it and, after I nodded, asked, "Do you really think that a book tells you what you need to know about what I do and why?"

I caught myself before responding, recognizing that, yes, I'd come to that book as a reader hoping for insights into adolescent literacy practices (both in and outside of school), but also that he had a significant point. He continued with a question that I eagerly pursued, "What do you want to know?"

Doug and I sat down in the library (it was his study period) and talked at length about the tools he used (ranging from his page on Facebook to the iPod that was attached to earbuds threaded throughout his backpack so as to keep them from tangling but also from being seen by adults in the building), his motivation for engaging within those spaces, and, important to me, the ways in which he is learning to read and write in digital spaces. Our discussion, and discussions I had with several students in this and other schools, follow, interwoven with current research, ideas about how we think about the skills/literacies/tools that digital youth bring into our classrooms, and an examination of how these ideas are reflected and captured in the AL Brief.

Listening to our students and paying particular attention to the literacies that they bring into our classrooms isn't a new or even twenty-first-century practice. For me, this work isn't driven by the need to think about new technologies and media. It is steeped in practice, in thinking about connecting with adolescents, no matter whether they are particularly "plugged in." I try not to get locked up in terms like *digital natives* or *millenials* for a variety of reasons, the most important of which is that they cloud my thinking with ideas about technologies and cyberskills over the work of seeing actual kids. As an English teacher, my interest lies in students' literacy practices (e.g., development of voice, sharing ideas within a network, constructing meaning across media, engaging in a community by putting knowledge to work and into action), as it was before computers came into my classroom. It isn't "new" literacies *or* "old," just as we aren't "digital natives" versus "digital immigrants." We are all learners in a literacy landscape that is unfamiliar but packed with new possibilities.

What the Data Say

Multiple studies have emerged over the past five years investigating what adolescents do outside of schools when engaged with new media. Looking across the findings of the Pew Internet Group's work since 2005, the Kaiser Foundation's 2005 study of "Generation M," and those of the Digital Youth Project at Harvard University's Berkman Center, big ideas emerge, providing us with insight into the level of use/saturation of youth media practices, the ways in which students and kids use social and creative media, and the role that networks/communities have made possible and leveraged.

For many of our students, online access is a given, whether they are connecting from a computer or a mobile device. Current work from the Pew Internet and American Life Project indicates a continuing increase in the number of youth (ages 12–24) who are online, jumping to 93 percent when examined between November 2007 and February 2008 (Lenhart et al., "Writing"). One hundred percent of public schools now have Internet access, and current estimates hold that schools average at least one computer for every four students (Tapscott 15). When online, digital youth typically engage in more than one digital medium at a time (e.g., listening to a lecture streamed online while reading source material) (Tapscott 106). And, as comes as no surprise to those of us who work in schools, the digital divide remains alive and well for students who come from low-income African American and Hispanic families (Rideout, Roberts, and Foehr 12).

Multiple studies (Pew Internet; Kaiser Foundation; Palfrey and Gasser) have demonstrated that the majority of online teens are using the Internet for more than simply accessing/pulling down information. Examined through the lens of the English classroom, their online practices can be grouped into three main categories: content creation, information production and use, and interacting within a community/network.

[handwritten margin note: 3 categories of Internet — ELA lens]

Content Creation

[handwritten note: arrow]

Internet use for digital youth is as much about pushing content up online as it is about pulling content down. A 2007 Pew Internet and American Life study held that 64 percent of online U.S. teens had created some sort of content on the Internet (Lenhart et al.). This work spans a significant range, including but not limited to uploading photos into photo sharing/editing tools such as Flickr or Photobucket; editing an article on Wikipedia; composing original writing in a fanfiction website; creating a video or remix posted to YouTube; or programming a new iPhone application. (If these terms are not familiar to you, don't worry. See the glossary at the end of the book for a short description of these and others.) Findings included:

- Thirty-three percent of online teens create or work on webpages or blogs for others, including those for groups they belong to, friends, or school assignments.
- Twenty-eight percent have created their own online journal or blog.
- Twenty-seven percent maintain their own personal webpage.
- Twenty-six percent remix content they find online into their own creations (Lenhart et al. i)

Palfrey and Gasser attribute the burst of creative productivity to the low cost of tools such as digital cameras and technology tools such as iMovie, which simplify the composing and remixing process, and the ease in locating/sharing peer-created content through tagging in ubiquitous sites like de.licio.us and Flickr (122–123).

Creativity with digital media presents opportunities for self-expression and remaking of content to meet a different goal/story/purpose/commentary. As Palfrey and Gasser share, "Young people are not passive consumers of media that is broadcast to them but rather active participants in the meaning-making of their culture" (131). Along with content creation comes a need to understand and work within copyright law, a literacy of increasing importance given the proliferation of online file sharing and remixing. Further, there is evidence that digital youth are increasingly aware of the need to restrict access to their posted work (Lenhart et al.).

As much as we celebrate the multimodal creativity demonstrated by students who are composing and creating online content, it is important to note that there remains a considerable number of students who aren't included in these numbers. Studies that looked at online teens, for example, showed that more than a quarter of teens who were online weren't engaging in any kind of creation. When we consider the digital divide, as much as our focus is typically centered on access to hardware/speedy Internet connections, Web 2.0 practices, such as content creation, establish an additional layer of the divide. So, as much as the divide is often measured by access to specific tools, we need to also consider the practices used even when tools are made available.

 ## Information Use

Digital youth are a generation marked by unprecedented access to information. Studies conducted by the Pew Internet and American Life Project reveal that more than three-quarters of teens aged 12–17 search online to access information about current events (Lenhart et al., "Teen"). That reflects a trend across the population as 45 percent of online users report that information found online was significant in their decision making (Horrigan and Rainie 1). And, just as with any other fluency, those students who spend the most time online and engaging thoughtfully with content are more critical of the information they find (Palfrey and Gasser).

Alongside the abundant information at students' fingertips is a change in how we look at the Internet. In its early stages, the Internet resembled a file cabinet, full of information that we pulled down. Now, given the capacity and nature of participatory media, digital youth engage in information *making* practices, seeing the Internet as a place for both pushing up and pulling down content (Tapscott 114).

This is evident in their practices in gathering and interacting with news and current events information found online. Palfrey and Gasser identify a three-step approach used by sophisticated digital youth as they gather and vet information. Beginning with the work of "grazing" (i.e., looking across search tools, including RSS aggregators, to locate content), digital youth, once at a point of saturation and confidence, move more deeply "to make sense of the news, to put it into a frame or better context, to offer an analysis of it, to introduce relevant other voices" (242). The final stage is the "feedback loop," in which readers share the information (and their perspectives) with one another through blog posts, microblogging, posting stories to social networking sites, etc. In the publishing of their ideas, they closely engage with and possibly even remake content, but, more important to the eventual step to "information creation," they begin to develop an expert voice. From here, it is a smaller move to edit a Wikipedia article, create a new resource, etc.

Just as in the discussion of what we know about digital youth's work in producing content, those students who have access to tools *and* experiences in thinking critically about and with information are best positioned to successfully hone those skills (Palfrey and Gasser). And, when we consider the realities facing our students who lack access (to both technologies and the thinking processes needed in finding and unpacking online information), the gap that is the digital divide widens.

Networked Participation

Digital youth engage in social networking sites for multiple purposes, but what is striking about this work is the characteristics of the sites used for these interactions and the nature of students' engagement as readers, writers, and communicators. Social network sites are a part of a broader landscape of social media that function to connect users across time and space. Within these spaces, youth collaborate, play multiuser games (from computers, gaming systems, iPods), update statuses, tweet/microblog, and more. Social media have been a part of the Internet since its inception. What makes this current run of tools different now are the genres of tools that have emerged and the ways in which they bring users together (i.e., through friending, or by posting user-generated content).

Data on use are thin but compelling given the relative "newness" of both the tools and the practices. In a 2006 study, the Pew Internet and American Life

Project found that 55 percent of online teens (aged 12–17) self-reported having a profile within a social networking site (Lenhart and Madden). Li found that 80 percent of online teens (again aged 12–17) read/engaged within social networking sites, with more than half doing so at least weekly. The 2007 Project Tomorrow/Speak Up data indicate that where more than 50 percent of all high schools use communication and social networking tools, girls' use outpaces boys' use by an average of 12 percentage points (Project Tomorrow 2). Where all online teens are not engaging in social networking sites, participation is valuable within peer groups and in building social capital (boyd, "Why Youth"). Research has indicated that where low-income, African American teens are active participants within social networking sites (when compared to more affluent, white students), what differs is how they use the site (boyd 3). As researcher danah boyd finds, "When it comes to social network sites, there appears to be a far greater participatory divide than an access divide" (2).

The functionality of social networking sites typically includes but is not limited to the capacity to build a "home" page most regularly referred to as a "profile," the ability to locate and move within lists and communities of "friends" (all of whom have developed their own profile pages), and spaces for posting information (e.g., photos, links, notes, videos) and receiving feedback through comments and asynchronous and synchronous communication tools. The primary motivation for participation in a social network is to interact with friends and/or members of the community (Lenhart et al., "Teens and Social Media"). And the resulting profile "becomes yet another mechanism by which students can signal information about their tastes and identities" (boyd, "Why Youth"). Here, digital youth "write themselves into being" (Sundén 4) for what is deemed an "imagined audience" (boyd, "Why Youth") that is seemingly defined in size and composition by the user. While this is a type of publishing that blurs the lines between what is private and what is public, research indicates that digital youth are drawn to these spaces for much of the same identity-building capacity that former generations experienced in different, nondigital spaces (Ito et al.).

While the majority of digital youth use spaces like Bebo or Facebook to extend friendships, a small but growing number of youth "also use the online world to explore interests and find information that goes beyond what they have access to at school or within their local community" (Ito et al. 1). In other words, they use the spaces to extend their own learning through interest-driven participation. As Ito et al. explain, "Youth find a different network of peers and develop deep friendships through these interest-driven engagements, but in these cases the interests come first, and they structure the peer network and friendships" (14).

[handwritten margin note: Same w/ adults ie. me w/ education blogging community?]

Reading, Writing, Representing, and Engaging

Digital youth understand that the Internet allows what they create to be seen, heard, and used, and most are coming to learn how to leverage a community or network to extend their ideas, leading to "viral" content or feedback on remixed media. As much as these are opportunities for students to push back against the print-centric definition of literacy that is deeply embedded and most dominant in the English language arts curriculum, they are also opportunities for engaging with students and showing them how they are literate. In thinking about this in the context of my own teaching, I work with an increasing number of students who don't speak the traditional language of the classroom. But by creating a learning space where new media converges with traditional literacy practices (as opposed to "colliding with" in an either/or approach), I aim at creating a new space for more students to find success and to be intentional in choosing the media through which to express their thinking.

ELL implication

As I think about the creative or publishing roles associated with the use of those new media (especially as tools for extending understanding and communicating), I've found a 2008 report by Hannon et al. helpful. In it, they offer a graph (see Figure 2.1) that puts together the kinds of digital media that students encounter and work with along with the specific roles they engage in when working with those texts.

How does this graph help me to think differently about the English classroom? First, it challenges me reflect on the roles that a student might take on when

explanation of why this chart is helpful

1) Role of students
2) Role of schools

Figure 2.1: New media "types" and practices from *Video Republic* by Celia Hannon, Peter Bradwell, and Charles Tims. European Cultural Foundation Report. London: Demos, 2008. www.demos.co.uk.

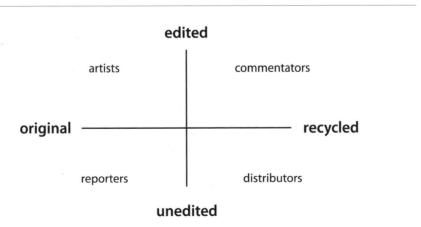

creating, publishing, or sharing digital media. Some of these feel familiar to an English classroom (e.g., helping students to develop voice as reporters), and others may present some new possibilities (e.g., helping students to decide which content they might want to distribute or share with others and asking them to think about what that work—in the role of the "distributor"—can mean). Further, it helps me to recognize that students are working with digital media that extend beyond their own original content. We engage in a different kind of writing and thinking when we are working with content that is recycled or when we are thinking about ways of remixing individual texts into something new. Point of view, for example, might take on a whole new meaning here. Copyright becomes increasingly complex.

Considerations for recycled work

Looking at this graph also helps me think about the role of schools. I believe that school needs to be a place where we're teaching students how to thoughtfully and purposefully engage in this work. My job as a teacher is to help students engage as critical readers of literary texts but also to help them unpack, examine, and engage in the literacy practices that new media make possible.

As captured in each of the roles depicted in this graphic, digital youth engage with media to learn, to develop a sense of identity and expertise, to express their ideas, and to engage in an attempt to "do" something, whether that be through collective action (e.g., in "mobs" gathered through Twitter) or social commentary (e.g., through a remix of political campaign footage). The English classroom that values new literacy practices needs to find ways to engage all students in that work and in thinking deeply and critically about what these new roles as writers and readers entail and open up.

Meeting and Listening to Digital Youth

As much as I learn from close reading of emerging research on the practices and literacies of digital youth, I like to anchor my thinking to dialogue with the kids I work with both in school and at out-of-school programs. What follows is a discussion of the literacy practices of three adolescents who use new media in specific ways, some of which echo the research and others of which challenge some findings in interesting ways. Again, my goal as a researcher was to learn new ways of seeing, valuing, and leveraging the digital "funds of knowledge" (Moll et al. 134) they bring into our English classroom. I did so by having individual discussions and interviews with the students, observing their work in the classroom, reading their profiles and other documents that are a part of their "digital footprint," and observing/participating in learning contexts outside of school (e.g., an after-school digital storytelling program). Further, I anchor each story to the specific context in which the student identified his or her digital work as having the most energy, impact, and meaning.

Molly: Being Digital in School

Molly is a sixteen-year-old student at Richland High School, a rural school with
a total student population of five hundred students, grades 9–12. During seventh
period, she is enrolled in Honors 11 English with Mrs. Scott (and thirty-two classmates). While the curriculum in the course is fairly traditional (e.g., reading mostly
canonical American literature, multiple opportunities for expository writing,
extensive state assessments examining reading comprehension and understanding
of language), students are asked to create individual or group projects at the end of
each unit that both synthesize their learning and present an artifact. For example,
at the close of a unit on the American Dream (in which students read *The Great
Gatsby* and *Fences*), Molly worked with three peers to develop a collection of oral
histories capturing the way that three generations within a local family understood,
articulated, and pursued their American Dreams.

Molly does have access to technology both at home and at school, though
she often works with equipment and/or connections that she identifies as outdated
or slow. At home, she has access to her own Mac laptop (which she describes as
a hand-me-down, as it is an older model MacBook) and a dial-up connection. At
school, most of her classrooms have one networked computer, with all but two of
these functioning as dedicated "teacher stations." All English and business classes
have access to two shared, networked computer labs with thirty PCs in each. The
school library/media center also has a small number of digital cameras, voice re-
corders, and video cameras available for student and teacher use.

Describing Digital Practice

Molly managed to integrate technology into each of the culminating unit projects
she completed while also threading it into her practices in locating information,
reading connected or connective texts, discussing literature, and even communicating with peers about assignments, tasks, and questions that emerged while they
were reading. When asked to explicitly identify tools or discuss her motives behind
selecting them for a particular task, she resisted, explaining, "The only time that I
find myself thinking about technology is when it isn't there to do what I'd like or
when I have a teacher like you asking me to draw it out. If I have to think about
it, that means it is getting in the way of what I really want to be doing." That said,
once she started to draw out the list of tools she used most regularly to support her
learning or to create/compose, she identified Gmail, Google Documents, Voice-
Thread, de.licio.us, Skype, Moodle (for those courses that had developed sites),
communities within Ning, and Twitter.

For the first project of the year, Mrs. Scott asked students to write about the
most compelling book they'd ever read. While some students chose to present

[handwritten margin notes: rural, limited technology example (but the student uses multiple technologies); important to keep in mind; technologies she uses; Student choice in type of presentation → choice; exposure to variety → choice]

their work through a reflective essay, others chose to use PowerPoint or iMovie to create multimedia presentations. Molly chose to develop a VoiceThread composition in which she interwove still images with her spoken narration. So, instead of writing a five-paragraph essay, she offered twelve images, some of which showed her reading the actual book and others that represented the images she envisioned as she read. Wrapped around those twelve images were her thoughts and ideas, spoken aloud as each image appeared on the screen. To her, this was the project that set her creativity in motion: "Where I'd done this before, I'd never done it for a class. I did it to play around after a youth group trip—but here I used it to think about my reading. I didn't write it from start to finish. Instead, it emerged as I included the images and bits of narration. I liked writing that was more open and more responsive." The rubric Mrs. Scott had designed had allowed for creativity in presentation, but Molly found it didn't leave enough space/room for the kinds of formative feedback she wanted. As a result, she shared the URL for her project, inviting Mrs. Scott to comment within the project. Molly explained, "I didn't do that to teach her to use VoiceThread . . . though I think I did. . . . It was more about using the tool the way that anyone does. It isn't just about what you can express. It's about how others interact with it that matters."

Because she is a fairly organized student, one of Molly's sources of frustration during class projects is the challenge of working in groups to accomplish a task. As she explained, "It isn't that I don't want to or like to work. I just go a little nuts when everything is everywhere—which really means that we have nothing and it isn't anywhere." When reading *The Adventures of Huckleberry Finn*, students worked in large teams on a mock trial project. To facilitate the work within her group of six (assigned to developing the case for the prosecution), Molly suggested that they use Google Documents to store (and collaborate on) the many pages of text that they were writing as well as the set of links anchoring much of their online research. She offered, "I hadn't used it before, but it was just like Word. The only paper we needed was individual stuff. So if someone was absent, we were still okay. We'll just say that the other groups weren't so lucky." Molly was surprised by how efficient the work was, as "I'd expected we'd get blocked, but the site wasn't filtered, and we were able to jump on quickly as everyone has a Google account." As Molly talked about this experience, she emphasized that she wanted me to think about something bigger than the tool. She offered, "The deal here isn't that I used a technology. It is that I used a technology to be smarter in school. There is an important difference there."

During the fourth grading quarter, students were required to create anthologies of poetry that engaged them as readers, resonated with their experiences, or were useful models for their own writing. While some of her peers used presentation software to develop electronic anthologies pairing images with text and, in some cases, sound track, Molly went a different route, explaining that "[m]y technology for this is a notebook because, as a writer, I like to hear how the pen scratches, and I want to put it in my pocket and go. So if I use a tool, it has to do something else."

As she collected the texts that she enjoyed the most as a reader, Molly noticed that all but one were written by contemporary poets and that her reflective writing was mostly a collection of questions about writer's craft, intentionality, and how language worked and emerged in the texts. After randomly looking up one of her favorite poets on MySpace, she noticed an email link. Molly explained, "I immediately thought, 'Oh, do it.' If she was actually getting this email, I might be able to actually talk with her about her writing and the questions I couldn't figure through." Her email was answered that night. In thinking back on that moment, Molly offered, "I think I honestly hit the refresh button on my screen as if that would bring it faster, and, when it did come, I was surprised that it wasn't just a form 'thanks for your email' email." Molly was able to share her questions and ideas and, more important, she did so in dialogue with a poet whose work had captured her interest and imagination.

Molly's final poetry anthology was a multimodal text in which she included a bound, print copy of the collection of poems, each marked up with her notes and annotations; a printed copy of her email exchanges with three poets she had located online; and a fifteen-minute video in which she brought together her written and, in one case, Skype discussions with the three poets. In thinking about what she learned within the project, Molly shared:

> I think I've figured out that the Internet works in two ways. First, I can use it to find the "fill in the blank" information that took me to the first step in my work . . . like finding the poems or where a poet wrote. Bigger, I can use it to move what I usually write in a notebook into opportunities to talk with writers about what they do. So, I get smarter either way, but talking with poets through Skype or email takes it to a whole new level.

Molly was the only one of her peers to develop this kind of a project, but her writing and reflections led Mrs. Scott to use her project artifacts as a model for future semesters of students. Rightly so, Molly was quite proud of her accomplishments over the course of the term, celebrating that she'd moved in two different ways: one, as a student of literature, writing, and language, and two, as a literate communicator who discovered and used tools that helped her work and learn.

Learning How

In each case, Molly's work with technology did not emerge from an explicit requirement or activity modeled or experienced in class. Instead, each instance that

assess technology & students know how to use and open up opportunities to utilize in projects

she discussed grew out of a merging of what she wanted to learn or do and the ways in which a tool or technology would allow her to attain those goals. She spoke of this in terms of identity, offering, "I know that I'm a smart student and that I have resources I can access to do more, write more, understand more, read more. I like to play. And, if I play with a new tool and it doesn't work, it's not a big deal because the tool fails, not me."

She took pride in being largely self-taught when it came to the work of locating and learning the specific tools she used both in and outside of the classroom. "Let me be straight, though," she shared. "I'm no technology person. No clue how anything actually works. But I am motivated to figure out what might work. To me, that is different." Of importance to Molly were the ways she could be a better writer, as opposed to the ways she could be a savvier computer user. She explained, "I am more than happy to find and figure through something new if and only if I see something within it before I even start—and it has to come to me as a reader— and it has to come to me as a writer. This still is school." She was consistent in emphasizing that while she had yet to learn a tool at school that she hadn't previously used, she did learn new possibilities with the tools she already knew when the assignments were open enough for her to follow her thinking.

As much as Molly researched, located, and learned tools on her own, especially when driven by her needs and interests, she also spoke of the importance of peers and others who use or model the uses for new tools, ideas which she then builds on in her own practice. She explained, "A sign here should read 'cliché ahead,' but I can't do this without the people around me. I have friends who write and work in ways similar to me, and, as most of what we use are social tools, we learn them when communicating." Molly spoke to the talents of some of her specific peers:

> We don't all have to know all of the tools in order to really know how to use technology. So, you talk about digital natives. . . . It isn't like there are kids walking around who know everything. Instead, we each know something about a range of things and come together to know what we can know next.

Teaching a Teacher

Molly did speak to feeling uncomfortable when integrating technology into her classroom work or projects in a way that a teacher might not have expected (or known). She explained, "I get shot down sometimes because teachers don't think outside of what they have already done or come to see. I don't push for a bunch of reasons . . . but I take any chance to show what I know or am coming to know." English class with Mrs. Scott was one of Molly's favorite classes as "[s]he lets me work in the ways that fit me, and gives me feedback on what is working in terms of my writing or reading . . . so she isn't hung up on how or where I write but, instead, what I have to say." Molly is a skilled reader and writer, but she was adamant that her success in the classroom (and that of her peers) hinged on the teacher. "It's about seeing how I am a reader and a writer—if that doesn't happen, I play school and my peers just tune out."

In articulating her needs, Molly was clear in emphasizing, "I need school to be a place that is different from what it is now." She spoke of teachers' assumptions ("They think we won't or can't do homework that involves technology but don't see that it is the homework assignment that is the problem. When it matters, we can make it happen."), issues of access ("It doesn't help me if we have one computer in the room and it is tied and locked to the teacher desk."), and the difference between using a technology that is assigned and a technology that is chosen ("If I can make the choice, I can do more with it. If I can't, chances are I don't do much because it becomes about the tool and not what I need to do my work.").

Access issues abound within her school. Students don't have access to computers on a regular basis but, according to Molly, there is a larger problem. "My ideas come," she explained, "when I am in the classroom and I have to hold onto them as I can't go into the lab in that moment. And no matter how good I am at keeping notes, I usually lose that by the time I revisit." As another layer to the problem, the school network is "protected" with a strict firewall that blocks the majority of the Web 2.0 sites (e.g., Flickr, Ning) that Molly seeks to compose in, interact with, and work on. Unfortunately, "I can't choose what's on the machines, but there is also no process for me to make suggestions or even to be trusted." Her strategy for addressing this is also not supported in her current school context—use of her smart phone. She shared, "I can do more with what I have on my phone than I can on a school computer. I'm open about it and am happy to show what I'm doing. I'm not texting. I'm online. I'm composing. And once I do, I can use what I've done to advocate for opening it up. That doesn't make a lot of sense, but it is what I have to do."

Lily: Being Digital at Home

Lily is a sophomore at Western Senior High School, enrolled in "standard" English 10 as this is her first term in a U.S. school and English is her third language (behind Zulu and Portuguese). A recent immigrant from Johannesburg, South Africa, she works hard, and her sights are set on moving into an honors-level course at the start of the next semester. Lily explained, "I needed to be in this class to get my English moving. I had it, but I didn't do it enough for it to be as [fast] as I need it to do school well here." The high school is only three years old and has a dedicated computer lab for the English department and four wireless laptop carts.

Each classroom has a SmartBoard. Further, teachers' English curriculum guides have suggested websites and technology-integrated activities built into each unit.

Technology is a major part of Lily's home life, as each family member has his or her own laptop complete with a webcam that is used to interact with family in South Africa and across the globe through Skype or iChat. She explained, "I don't see the technology at home as we all have it and it isn't bigger than what the telephone with a cable on the wall is to my parents." She identified a central difference between technology at home and at school that is useful in considering how she works in both environments: "It's just different. In the school, teachers tell me how to be on. At home, I lead that with what I want to do. In the school, teachers get stuck on the technology where I get stuck on the saying or the doing."

Describing Digital Practice

Lily is an active technology user outside of school, ranging from her use of Twitter, iChat, Skype, and Bebo to stay in touch with peers to producing and sharing her own art (posted in Flickr and developed with tools like Photoshop). An avid photographer, Lily spoke of using her camera to navigate her new home:

> I started in photography when we went climbing or camping back home. Then, I used it to document what I saw when they started cutting down trees to build houses. . . . Here, the landscape is new to me. I use my lens to see it, and then to see me in it.

New to Baltimore, Lily posted her images in Flickr.com in order to house, tag, and organize them, but, more important, to share what she was seeing and experiencing with friends and family. As an unintended benefit of opening her pictures to any viewer in Flickr.com, Lily began to receive feedback and comments from other photographers, from residents in the communities she "read" with her lens, and from others who came to her work through searches for related or specific tags. Audience was a benefit and a challenge as Lily explained, "What was once just for me grew. Not bad or good. Just different . . . and bigger."

Her work moved to another stage as she started a blog in Wordpress. Initially, she used the blog as a place for writing about her photos, reflecting on their composition, how she used them to see the home she was making in the United States, the changes or patterns she saw in looking across them, etc. And the community watching her work in Flickr moved with her, offering longer, more detailed feedback and comments, sharing their own images in response, and challenging her to develop her language skills as quickly as possible. She explained, "I had to write and it was bumpy. I had to read and that was bumpy, too. But now, I practiced. It took a long time to read, look up translation, and write, but the more I did it, the more I picked up." Whereas Lily came to the blog thinking that she'd post every couple of weeks, she quickly found herself writing almost daily, through both

TWT –
comments
fuel us

original posts and responses to the comments her work and ideas received. She explained, "Comments keep me moving ahead, and I like that."

The third step for her work came from a suggestion by a peer commenter. "A reader in Los Angeles who came here from Sudan wanted to see me share, visually, what I wrote about, even things I couldn't post, like a handout from school." The reader recommended that Lily vlog by posting through recorded video. This upped the stakes since "I can fix mistakes when I print them. I can't do that on a video unless I edit, and vlogs do not usually do that." She sat on the idea for a few weeks until she wanted to share a certificate of achievement she'd won at a community art festival. So, for her first vlog entry, she held up the certificate and offered a three-minute "thank you" to the readers/commenters on her blog and Flickr postings.

Each of her three steps toward using technology to better communicate and develop her ideas and skills was motivated by a need to connect with a community that was invested, connected, and peer. This reached a new height with the vlog post, and by posting it on YouTube and embedding it into her blog, Lily invited even more participation and feedback, as viewers could comment in YouTube and/or on her blog. She shared, "It didn't go viral, but more people saw it and me. . . . I like seeing how my ideas can spread. I'm not on unless it needs to happen, unless I have something I have to say . . . but, when I do, my readers and peers are all there."

Learning How

Lily didn't learn how to use Flickr, Bebo, Wordpress, or YouTube from her time in the classroom. In fact, she found that idea to be comical. "It hasn't been long, but I think that if I had to wait for it to come in school, it would be done by that point. Technology in school isn't about connecting or really doing anything. It is about doing an assignment." This wasn't a reflection that was limited to her time in the U.S. system; it was a blanket statement across all of her formal schooling.

Learning the tools that supported her work was a process of thinking about what she wanted to do, the suggestions offered by the community of friends and readers who engaged with her work (whether in Flickr or in her eventual blog), and play. As she offered, "I do not learn about technology from a guide or help menu. I learn by thinking with my fingers on the keyboard." And, as she emphasized regularly, "This isn't about the tool as much as it is about what I wanted to say with my photographs and my words. The technology *had* to do that." In those instances when she couldn't work her way through what she wanted a tool to do, she relied on technologies like email or Skype to connect her with the voices and screens of those "peer teachers" who were the closest to her work. She explained, "It helps to talk online with my readers and friends as they know my languages, both the words and the commands in the technology."

Teaching a Teacher

Where Lily's initial work in posting her photos on Flickr was motivated by her goal to connect as an individual to the environment around her, her motivation to blog and vlog was fed and amplified by the connection to the community of peers and readers who responded to and pushed the thinking within each post. Audience in her work outside of school went well beyond what she knew in school, where her work was read and assessed almost exclusively by teachers. In the two weeks when she recorded her reflections on her uses of technology, her blog received 12,500 hits and thirty-seven new comments in response to her ideas.

Lily's writing in the blog/vlog was rich in voice, perspective, and reflection. As much as she wrote with the knowledge that "someone" was reading, at its core, her writing supported her discovery of place, of language, and of connections within a community with shared interests. That said, she wrote from her expertise—her experiences as an adolescent, a South African, and a photographer navigating a new culture, a new language, a new school, and a continually new community interested in watching her work unfold. She explained the importance of the "expert voice" present in her blog: "I am present here in the ways I can't be present in a prompt. In school, I write to perform. Here, I write to figure things out and to belong to something bigger."

As a writer, Lily wanted to discuss how her writing process outside school worked. "In the classroom, we follow a plan, write, revise, write, publish, and process. In my real writing, I think, write, link, revise, post, respond. It is really different, but I think I get a better end." Just as a poster in Lily's English classroom depicted a nonlinear, recursive writing process, the "steps" depicted were different from what she experienced in writing outside of the classroom. She had explicit needs from her English teacher: "This is about language for me, but it is also coming to know how to be a writer with something to say. I need to know how the two different models fit together. Should they? Do they?" Lily expected her English teachers to be skilled at more than just writing print text. She expected English teachers to write across technologies and spaces, to be able to make connections and teach writers across modes and media.

Andrew: Being Digital within a Community

Andrew is an eighth-grade honors student at City Middle School where all students have access to three computer "hubs" of twelve computers each in the media center as well as multiple laptop carts that are shared across grade-level teams. Most classrooms have LCD projectors or ActivBoards. As in most schools, technology use hinges on the instructional practices and interests of specific classroom teachers. Andrew describes his English and social studies teachers (who co-teach a "humanities block") as "technology-interested" and regular users of PowerPoint. The current school policy forbids students from bringing their own laptops, cameras, or cell phones into the school.

Outside school, Andrew shares a family computer with his 11-year-old brother and his parents. That said, during the two weeks that students were asked to "log" their uses and hours, Andrew engaged in a broad range of digital spaces (e.g., MySpace) and activities (e.g., online multiplayer games) and accrued an average of three hours per day online. He explained, "I don't really think of it as going online. It's just play, or talking with my friends. I don't actually think of the computer at all, just of the thing I want to do."

Describing Digital Practice

One of the interdisciplinary units embedded into the eighth-grade curriculum tasks students with conducting oral histories of elders in their community. For their culminating unit project, Andrew and his peers were asked to interview men and women who had rich memories of World War II, through either the ways in which it impacted them as "participants" (which the teachers defined as being directly involved in events of the war) or as "bystanders" (which the teachers defined as an acute awareness of what was occurring, but through a distance or participation in new job opportunities for women or food rations). The only technology involved in the unit (as written) was students' use of a tape recorder and a word processor for transcribing and writing up their findings.

Andrew was captivated by the assignment, explaining, "I'm a good student, but I typically see school as just that . . . in school only. This was different. It was in school and all around me." His interviewee was an eighty-five-year old Holocaust survivor who shared stories about her experiences in Poland as a young child. Andrew was deeply engaged both with coming to know her and in accurately and powerfully capturing her story and experiences. He explained a frustration that emerged as he engaged in the work: "This is work that could really matter, and it's staying stuck in a shoebox of audiotapes and a printout of a paper. For a lot of us, our work couldn't have been less about the grade."

He approached his teachers about extending the project or doing something different with their projects but was frustrated that the responses he received were focused on instructional time and what teachers saw as enough opportunity for sharing through an end-of-unit "reading" of students' work. Thinking of possibilities and still frustrated, an idea came to Andrew as he was watching a video that had gone viral on YouTube, "David Back from the Dentist." He explained:

> So, this is a video of a little kid doped up on something they gave him at the dentist— and it has hundreds of thousands of views. I'm writing an oral history of a hero, and it

will be lucky to have four readers—me, her, my teacher, and my mom. That sucks. So, I started thinking outside of school.

Working with several friends in the class (and with the permission of their interviewees), Andrew digitized his tape-recorded audio and shared it as a podcast on a blog they created to house their work. Within a weekend, they had posted eight interviews paired with their descriptive and reflective writing and some comments on one another's work. In an attempt to bring more classmates to the site, Andrew shared the URL in a post to his Twitter account. As a result of his efforts and those of his peers, their work came together in a blog sharing oral histories and interviews of community members and the comments, understandings, and ideas of adolescents who were coming to know and see their community in new ways.

Andrew wasn't satisfied as he saw their work as only shifting in medium. "The only change here was that we were writing on digital paper, which has the benefit of attracting audience, but you have to know it is there to even find it." His focus, and that of his peers, shifted from thinking about the tools (which is what the work in moving to podcasts and blogs had really been) to thinking about people. As Andrew explained, "I can publish for free when I'm online. There are hundreds of ways to do it. And I had to change my approach from thinking about how to why. I wanted to share stories and perspectives for others to engage but also to capture something unique to our community."

He approached a librarian at the community library and pitched an idea to use a computer for viewing/sharing the students' oral histories. She agreed, providing that the resource was high quality and that they had secured permissions from any participants. To that end, Andrew and a crew of eight peers used the following weekend to create a site using a mash-up tool that brought together audio files and placed them on a Google Map that could be published or password-protected. He explained, "The Google Map was about organizing our files and sharing ideas about location. The interviewees lived in specific pockets of our community, and we wanted to show that."

In reflecting on what brought Andrew and his peers to develop this project from what had originally been assigned in school, Andrew shared, "We needed to do something with what we'd done and the questions it pushed us to think about." He was completely surprised that this was work that was interesting and motivating to his peers. He explained, "Together, it's like we are creating what's possible."

Learning How

Like the other digital youth described in this chapter, Andrew had to work to identify more than a handful of technologies that he had been "taught" to use. In his words, "If you're teaching me to use a tool, I take that to mean that we're sitting together, talking about where to click, working step by step . . . and I've only ever done that when I was in a typing class in elementary school . . . with keyboarding software." Given the onslaught of new tools that are rapidly developed and shared online, he spoke of the importance of what he called "staying open." He shared:

> It just happens—the suggestion of the right tool at the right time. If I go hunting for it, I might find it—but if I use something like Twitter, I work alongside others who are likely already using it. I don't have to do it on my own. There are other seekers out there doing that part.

When thinking about the role that school and teachers could play in this work, Andrew offered little but did emphasize that he needed models and open thinking. As he explained, "I want my teachers to blog and work with new tools. So, if you're teaching me history, do it so I can see how you use these tools [to do your work]." He wanted teachers to model not where to point and click but how to use tools to be skilled scholars, writers, and readers. When doing so, "Teachers would then help me to see what is possible, not about a tool. . . . We're wasting time if we're talking about where to click. I'm not sure teachers get that."

Teaching a Teacher

Andrew's reflections on his work centered on community, the neighborhood community that benefited from and accessed the oral history audio map, the community of peers who helped take the project to a new place, and the online community that supported and challenged their growth. This was a community that came together for authentic reasons. So, moved by shared interests and a tool set that allowed them to come together (the blog, Twitter, or the audio map), they were able to accomplish what was a shared goal. And they did so through a cycle of doing, seeing what happened, seeing new possibilities, and then doing something else. This isn't a "finished" project, as is also captured in that cycle.

What does that mean for teaching? This was work that started in the classroom and clearly had rich potential for meaning something *outside* of the classroom. Seeing those opportunities to ratchet up the relevance of our students' work is difficult but critical to what we know about motivation and engagement. Further, an invested, authentic community supported the work. Feedback came from those who were helping to create, helping to populate, and helping to disseminate the audio map, and not from a single classroom teacher. Technology was used to bring people together, through both their stories and their varied contributions to the project. Moving these ideas into our instructional practice is a big challenge, which certainly can't happen in every unit and at every grade level. But, as I'll discuss in later chapters, these are ideas that we can integrate into practice at key moments to amplify our pedagogies and, more important, student engagement and learning.

Making Meaning across Student Stories

It never fails. I am continually surprised by the multiple ways in which kids show us how they are smart and how they are literate. Choosing these three stories meant weeding through countless other examples of student work that demonstrate how digital youth are working as readers, writers, speakers, artists, and composers in compelling, important ways. And, looking into your own classroom, you likely have your own stories to share. When I look across the work and ideas of these adolescents through the lens of the AL Brief and the research discussed earlier in the chapter, I see three foundational patterns (and hope that you see even more).

First, *digital youth are engaging in literacy practices that are richly multimodal*. In just these three examples, students are writing in blogs, wikis, podcasts, interactive Google maps, mash-ups, micro-blogging sites, online participatory communities, social networking spaces, and more. And, as the brief espouses, "Research on reading and writing beyond the classroom shows that students have literacy skills that are not made evident in the classroom unless teachers make special efforts to include them" (2). This presents real challenges in English language arts classrooms as it requires that we open up our texts, assignments, and assessments in ways that allow students to engage in multiple modes and media.

Second, *these varied literacy practices allow students to work in different roles*. They are not solely readers and writers. As Hannon et al. argue, students are working with content that is original, edited, unedited, and recycled. Molly's poetry anthology engaged her as an artist and commentator. Lily's blog offered her work as an artist, a commentator, and a reporter. Andrew took on the roles of distributor and commentator as he and his friends developed the interactive audio map of their community oral histories. These are important twenty-first-century roles that are implicitly present in our standards documents and curricular guides but that need skillful teasing out in order to become meaningful in our practice and student learning.

Finally, *community-building is at the core of our work as English teachers* as we work to develop a community in our classrooms that supports both the work of literary interpretation and writers' craft. Doing so apart from the community practices students try out in social networks is what posits our work as "school" as opposed to work that is just what smart, invested thinkers do when they come together around shared interests and goals. That doesn't mean that all of our classrooms need to jump onto Facebook. Each of these digital youth emphasized the importance of the tool set as existing simply to bring people together to do something. The AL Brief emphasizes, "Adolescents regularly use literacies for social and political purposes as they create meanings and participate in shaping their immediate environments" (3). As I think about what this means for teaching, I have to push past the stereotype telling me that students are "always on" to accomplish social goals as opposed to intentionally using tools to gather, compose, and make meaningful work happen. Last, as discussed in later chapters, I have to think deeply about ways to involve and engage *all* my students in this work, not just those with backgrounds and literacy environments that are continually telling them that this work is possible.

**Chapter
Three**

The Twenty-First-Century English Teacher

All learning pivots on who we think we are, and who we see
ourselves as capable of becoming.

         —Frank Smith

The introduction of a transformative technology into the
classroom will be and should be evolutionary.

         —Ewa McGrail

Teaching in a Digital Age

Lately, when working with groups of secondary English teachers, I typically
begin by polling the group to identify whether they are *digital natives*. I find it
interesting that no matter where I am, Texas or Manitoba, the same thing plays
out. A small number of hands rise, and, predictably, they are the hands of the
younger teachers in the room who are likely to also be taking notes on a laptop,
a Netbook, or even an iPhone. The others in the room will label themselves
digital immigrants, the term for those of us who were born before 1986 (Tapscott 6–7) and would more likely carry something other than our laptops out of
our homes in the case of a fire (Aducci et al.).

As much as I bristle at either of these descriptors, there are complex ideas and assumptions within the thinking that they reflect. Embracing the role of the "immigrant" or the "Luddite" makes it too easy to hide behind language, cultural, and physical barriers. And it makes it too easy to forget that within every class of students or every room of teachers, some will have seemingly instinctive skills when it comes to working with new technologies and others will struggle to find the button to turn it on. Some will have SmartPhones with "always on" access, and others cannot afford a mobile phone, let alone a computer, in their homes. There isn't a level playing field, whether we are looking at the ways we plug in or, more important, the ways we create a space for the participation of those students or teachers who are not socially or financially privileged. It is a thickly complex problem.

As English teachers, our conversation needs to be situated intentionally and quite deliberately. At a point in the not-so-distant past, our thinking when a new computer or software program rolled into our classrooms left us asking, "What can I make this do?" Now, amidst almost continual change in what it means to read and write, our question needs to evolve to asking, "What do I *want* this tool to do?" When we get the question right, we can start focusing our thinking on examining how new technologies push up on what it means to learn—and how we think about it.

Teaching with New Literacies

As discussed in earlier chapters, Web 2.0 learning environments and practices *do* make possible opportunities for creating; for communicating in multiple modalities; for sharing and publishing our work for an engaged, invested audience; and for interacting and collaborating, even globally. The new literacy practices open up some new territory in the English classroom, while amplifying things that we'd previously known and embraced (see Table 3.1).

Table 3.1: Characteristics of Web 1.0 and Web 2.0 Practices

WEB 1.0	WEB 2.0
Individual	Collaborative, participatory
Print-based	Multimodal
Teacher- or curriculum-directed	Self-directed
Teacher-to-student feedback	Feedback from diverse publics, networks, collaborators
Receiving knowledge	Creating knowledge

Looking at this list in the context of what we do in our English classroom, "the place where students learn to master the power of words and symbols—theirs and others" (Applebee 73), I see immediately ideas about participation, composing through multiple modes and media, and engaging with authentic audiences.

None of these ideas are "new" to what it means to teach English. They are drivers behind our work in a writer's workshop, in creating collages of John Proctor's "open mind" at the end of act 2 of *The Crucible* (Burke 32) or maps of Huck Finn's journey down the Mississippi, and in actively discussing and constructing meaning from the texts we read. What is new is the opportunity to do this work with an expanded tool set, including but not limited to sharing image files, creating polls/surveys, blogging, participating in online projects, sharing audio files, and engaging with social networks. What is also new is doing so while critically thinking about our pedagogy and our learning, and how the tool allows us to amplify our teaching (Kajder, "Unleashing"; Kajder, "Tech-Savvy").

As captured in the AL Brief and the descriptions of adolescent literacy practices in Chapter 2, if we do this work in smart, intentional, and authentic ways, we can engage and grow students' skills as readers and writers in compelling fashion. This doesn't mean that we need to know, as users, where and how to point and click. It means that we follow the recommendations in the brief that remind us of how students need us and what we have to contribute (see list).

To do this work, we as teachers will have to constantly be learning. Again, this isn't limited to learning where to point and click. It is about learning new ways of engaging with media and developing literacies that move our own work as readers and writers. Once we "re-see" what it means to read and write, we can use those understandings to inform our practice. Harris argues that for a teacher to develop innovative, new pedagogies, the process is "additive, recursive, and expansive rather than a linear series of replacements of 'old' with 'new'"

Connections to NCTE's Adolescent Literacy Brief
Teaching with New Literacies/Web 2.0 Practices Can Impact . . .

1. **Motivation**

   "Adolescents rely on literacy in their identity development, using reading and writing to define themselves as persons." (2)

   "If they are not engaged, adolescents with strong literacy skills may choose not to read or write." (4)

2. **Language and Critical Thinking Skills**

   "Highly effective adolescent literacy teachers . . . teach with approaches that foster critical thinking, questioning, student decision-making, and independent learning." (5)

   "Learning the literacies of a given discipline can help adolescents negotiate multiple, complex discourses and recognize that texts can mean different things in different contexts." (3)

3. **Writing Skills**

   "Research shows that informal writing to learn can help increase students' learning of content material, and it can even improve the summative writing in which students show what they have learned." (2)

4. **Inquiry/Discovery**

   "Active, inquiry-based activities engage reluctant academic readers and writers." (4)

(269). Using the metaphor of a jazz performance, she argues that teacher learning and our resulting new pedagogies are "a well-practiced fusion of careful, creative planning and spontaneous improvisation" (251). This doesn't happen in an hour-long professional development lecture, but it can happen, over time, when we unpack our teaching, examine student learning, and look for openings for change.

There are very real and often loud voices that indict these efforts. Those arguments push that we pander to the tech-obsession of our digital youth, overemphasize twenty-first-century skills over the "foundational" ones of the nineteenth century (which many students have yet to master), and that the cost for this work is exorbitant (Bauerlein 10). That said, the counterarguments are just as compelling: that we pander to students through direct instruction and high-stakes assessments, that we need to redefine "basics," and that "old school" practices and methods don't motivate or engage student learning (Wesch, "Participatory"). As much as I might agree with both sides at varying points in their arguments, what keeps me firmly rooted in valuing and learning new literacy practices is that I want all of my students to be literate in the dominant media of their time. To do that today requires engaging with and in the media spaces and technologies available if only to complicate their work and perspective. Or, as Michael Wesch argues, "We [need to] use social media in the classroom not because our students use it, but because we are afraid that social media might be using them—that they are using social media blindly, without recognition of the new challenges and opportunities they might create" (n. pag.).

What is missing from the materials that I read to move and inspire teacher practice are models of smart teachers who are using (or not) Web 2.0 tools and new literacies practices within the English classroom and, as a result, moving (or not) students' learning. I find lots of data about what adolescents are doing outside of the classroom, or the kinds of tools that they use most regularly, but I don't see models of practice that help me to see what teaching with new technologies involves and makes possible. We don't get into our own heads enough when it comes to taking apart our practice, and we certainly don't have many models of teachers who make this practice accessible and "public." To that end, the examples that follow offer that critical examination of teachers' pedagogy and the literacy practices they foster and develop.

Meeting and Listening to Digital Teachers

As much as I learn from listening to and working alongside students, I also seek out smart English teachers who think deeply about their practice, their instructional goals, and the ways in which students grow and learn in their classrooms. Folding talk about new literacies and emerging technologies into the mix intensifies the discussion, in part because of the "urgency" to incorporate technology into our teaching (in some contexts) and in part because of the continual "newness" of that practice. To that end, what follows is an opportunity to listen in on three teachers as they discuss their practice, the ways in which it has (or hasn't) changed in response to new literacies practices and tools, and what looking at their teaching through the lens of the AL Brief teaches them.

Similar to the student stories, the voices and thinking in this chapter (and others) grew out of individual discussions/interviews, observations of teachers' work in the classroom, and examinations of examples of student work (digital and print). In what follows, I offer three portraits of teachers, loosely based on Palfrey and Gasser's typology for examining the ways in which new media impacts participants' literacy practices and work outside of the classroom as well as their pedagogy alongside their students. In this case, we'll look at Liz, a teacher who is "born digital and teaching digitally"; Brice, a teacher who is "not born digital but teaching digitally"; and Ed, a teacher who is "not born digital, but *learning* to live and teach digitally." By focusing on these teachers as "types," I hope to portray how they think about, design, and implement instruction meant to move students' learning as readers, writers, speakers, and thinkers.

Liz: Born Digital, Teaching Digitally

Liz teaches two sections of honors tenth-grade English and three sections of ninth-grade standard (on-level) English at Thayer High School. This is her third year of teaching, all at the same school and within the same grade level. She completed her student teaching in the same district in one of the feeder middle schools for Thayer High.

Her classroom is what she describes as "old school," given that it has two chalkboards and a single PC permanently anchored to her teacher's desk. While there are class-sized labs available for "reservation," because she is relatively new to the building (and low on the reservation list), she relies a great deal on her own laptop or the use of a laptop and projector that is regularly available through the library/media center. In her life outside of the classroom, she has a laptop that was required in her teacher education program, a digital camera, and a SmartPhone that she describes as "my lifeline when all the other things don't work." When thinking about her own uses of online tools, she named "Blogs, Twitter, Facebook . . . these are just my connecting. I don't think of them. . . . They are just there."

The Tools at Hand

When it comes to thinking about the tools she can access in her teaching, Liz looked outside of what the school can provide. She explained, "We have so little

. . . really. . . . I have to look harder or it would be really easy to not see what we could do." She started the year with opportunities for students to work with the classroom computer as part of a learning station, or with access to the lab when conducting research. That said, at the time when we met, she'd reached a place in the year and within the curriculum where she wanted both to engage in more participatory media and to build on the literacies that she knew kids were bringing into the classroom. As happens with so many of us when we mull over instructional plans, the idea emerged as she was working alongside a group of students on a completely unrelated project. She explained, "I was working on something else but was utterly distracted as I watched two students work to open their backpacks by untwining these long wires connecting their earbuds to their iPods. I started think-ing about what they were listening to—and there it was. . . . " The resulting project challenged students to develop their own audio content, to be streamed from a class podcasting site.

Although her classroom technology was far from cutting-edge, she recog-nized power in two things. One, she had a high-speed Internet connection that allowed for speedy file transfer and, more important to the activity, access to a network of potential collaborators and audience members. And, two, she had a strong relationship with her building technology coordinator who could easily be persuaded to allow downloads of free tools like Audacity, the audio-editing tool that would aid in creating students' audio projects.

As much as she needed to think about the technology resources she could access to make the project work, Liz emphasized that there was a more important "tool" for the work she was planning. She offered, "If I didn't have the space to create assessments and activities in my curriculum, and follow the guidelines as just that—guidelines—none of this would be possible." It was also helpful that, up through this assignment, her classes typically incorporated learning stations, studio spaces, and highly differentiated tasks. She explained, "If this was the first time I tackled all of those things, students would enter my class and think it was Pluto—and there would be no way I'd be doing any of them well because everything would be new. You've gotta have the core before you can be inventive."

In the Classroom

Liz designed an activity within her tenth-grade classes' unit on memoir/personal narrative. Initially, she'd planned to have students create podcasts of their memoir writing, but she wanted to take that to another level by disrupting the path be-tween student as writer and teacher as evaluator (or, in this case, listener). It was also important that she challenge students to consider divergent perspectives and experiences outside of what they'd know and see in their very small, very insular

site to collaborate with other classrooms

town. To that end, she posted a collaborative project to the class registry at Global SchoolNet, a website bringing together teachers and classes around specific projects posted to the site by teachers looking for collaboration.

Liz received responses from an eleventh-grade class in Kansas, a class of seventh and eighth graders in Oregon, and a tenth-grade class in Washington, DC. Together, Liz and the partner teachers crafted the assignment and the calendar/schedule of events. Modeling National Public Radio's StoryCorps work, students worked to write either their own story or capture the story of a close friend or family member—in response to a simple prompt asking them to tell a life story that needs to be captured and shared given the way it would/could resonate with or even teach listeners. Students recorded either the story or the interview, brought it to class on a jumpdrive or CD, and uploaded it to the class podcasting site. Then, across the four project sites, students shared and received feedback, critically evaluated the ways that the stories were constructed (and perhaps delivered).

Bringing Together Research and Practice

When Liz looked at this project against the ideas and research captured in the AL Brief, she struggled to narrow her response to specific lines of the document because "there was so much happening that I have all kinds of bells going off as I read particular sections of this." She centered her thinking on the instructional components that were both the roots and the outcomes of the work. She began by identifying what she saw as the start of her work, offering, "I had to start with my students, right? So, the brief talks a lot about valuing what kids bring. I did that literally by seeing the iPods and earbuds but in also thinking about why they were drawn to audio and how I could tap into that energy." She pointed to the line, "Teachers often devalue, ignore, or censor adolescents' extracurricular literacies, assuming that these literacies are morally suspect, raise controversial issues, or distract adolescents from important work" (3). Aware that students at Thayer High were not permitted to listen to iPods or MP3 players during school hours, Liz identified this as rooted in something bigger, suggesting that "[w]hen we tell kids they can't listen during school, we mean that they can't listen to something other than us. I wanted to shift that and say that they could listen to one another. . . . So take what might distract and use it to call our focus to kids' writing."

This was work that challenged students to be engaged, confident readers and writers as students worked across multiple "model" texts in order to better craft their own writing. Liz compiled a library of memoirs that students could work within, ranging from songs to podcasts, to images, to published print texts. More important to Liz was the variety of perspectives present across the texts as "[s]ustained experiences with diverse texts in a variety of genres that offer multiple perspectives on life experiences can enhance motivation, particularly if texts include electronic and visual media" (NCTE 4). Further, in working through the library of model texts, students were provided with an opportunity for choice and variety, each an opportunity for furthering their engagement with the task (NCTE 4).

As Liz read the brief, she continued to discuss the importance of real-world, authentic tasks. She offered, "It doesn't always happen this way, but students understood throughout this project that there was a big *why* behind our work. Unlike so many other things we ask for in school, this was a project or a product that did something outside of the classroom." For Liz and her students, the connections within this project happened across the library of texts students read and considered as writers, and, more important, the texts read and responded to within the project podcast site.

Liz also saw herself as a teacher within the pages of the brief, emphasizing the nature of her learning and engagement as both a teacher and a reader/writer. She explained, "So, I've taught this grade and curriculum for three years—and I keep thinking that I'll have it figured out and stable. But, as soon as I get confident, things change outside of the classroom, and I have to rethink." She kept circling around the statement "Literacy learning is an ongoing and non-hierarchical process" (2). It was complicated for her to unpack, but she offered:

evolving curriculum

> I'm so curious about what literacy is coming to mean that the "ongoing" part of it is daily for me, but the non-hierarchical part is where I really get it. If you tell me that audio texts don't "count," you are establishing a hierarchy that puts print texts ahead of other forms or modes, and you're further distancing the kids from the classroom who need a different kind of starting place. I had all kinds of participation in this project, and I don't think it was a coincidence.

Brice: Not Born Digital, Teaching Digitally

Brice teaches seventh-grade language arts at Valley Middle School, serving as team leader and coordinator of the after-school journalism program. He has taught English for twelve years: opening and teaching for four years at Valley Middle and for eight years in a nearby urban middle school. Given that Valley Middle is one of the newest and largest schools in the district, resources abound though class sizes average about twenty-seven students.

wider access to technology example

Brice's classroom is one of the few in the building with what he calls "flexible seating," a range of tables and chairs scavenged from across the building to support his continual rearrangement of the physical space of the classroom. His room contains an ActivBoard hanging at the front of the classroom and direct access to an adjoining computer lab scheduled only for the use of this seventh-grade team. The team also shares access to a set of ten digital cameras; five flip digital video cameras; and a box of miscellaneous microphones, external drives, and extra cables. Brice carries his MacBook laptop between home and school, preferring to do "everything" on the single machine that he backs up nightly. His learning is supported through engagement in the yearly K12 Online Conference, a fully online conference that brings together speakers from across the globe who are engaged with and committed to exploring the potential value added in emerging Web 2.0 technologies and, more important, pedagogies (http://k12onlineconference.org/). To identify Web 2.0 tools that others find useful and productive, Brice engages with a variety of media learning from podcasts developed by teachers across the globe, articles published in *Learning and Leading with Technology*, and social bookmarking tools.

The Tools at Hand

[handwritten margin note: while technology noted in standards]

During the academic year, Brice has interwoven podcasting, writing in iMovie, collaborative writing using wikis, and sharing writing with ePals, while always being driven by curricular goals and what he calls "the possibility in the tools in kids' hands." He has been pleased with students' work in each unit and activity, but he wants to take the final unit, focusing on short story writing, to a new place. In past years, students published print anthologies of their writing. As a result of students' work and relative successes with multimodal composing throughout the year, Brice now sees this project as a place for synthesizing their skills in communicating through multiple modes but doing so when the media could aid either in doing narrative work or in opening up new audiences or communities to students' writing.

Though our discussions about technology tools typically were centered in thinking about his students' work as readers and writers, Brice also regularly discussed his own learning. He offered, "As much as the kids are discovering and learning how to do this in class, I'm about a step ahead of them. So the technologies we use in class are tools for my learning as much as theirs as when I'm really there, I'm there before, during, and after the lesson." While Brice has abundant resources available for classroom use, he lacks teaching support because the building does not have a staff development teacher or instructional technology coach like those assigned to some of the other schools in the district.

In the Classroom

Brice's "reinvention" of the short story unit was designed to leverage the collaborative community students had worked all year to construct. As in all of his teaching, Brice took his time in thinking about where a technology might enrich student learning, considering both the skills that students were developing, the progress he'd like to see them make over the course of the instructional unit, and the new literacy practices that he'd like to engage. While he wanted to keep the class writers' workshop as stable as possible, he also wanted to involve students who still struggled with writer's confidence and provide access to new tools for receiving feedback and driving revision.

Writer's workshop context

This wasn't an overhaul of a unit. Instead, Brice built several small experiences meant to lead to a rich end product. He shared, "Doing work with technology isn't always about creating a huge, splashy end product and spending all of our time in a lab. Kids need to see what it is to select a tool to do something efficient, meaningful, and crisp. Where else will they learn that?"

Google Docs

At the start of the unit, students were instructed to post all writing in Google Documents, which facilitated sharing and receiving peer reviews and feedback. As a revision tool, students were asked to paste their text into wordle.net, a tool that generates a word cloud noting the words most regularly and least often repeated in the story. This yielded surprises: "It didn't go as well as I wanted as there were kids who apparently had an endless vocabulary and didn't repeat enough words. . . . But, for others, it was a wake-up call about rich language as words like 'good' or 'nice' were large and bold." Finally, he encouraged students to write across modes, taking advantage of the tools they'd explored throughout the year (e.g., Voice-Thread, Photoshop, Garage Band). Here, Brice offered, "I needed to give kids the permission to start here. Otherwise, they'd be stuck on a blank page or words that didn't do what they'd hoped to express." Finally, students' work was published through an electronic book, a multimedia presentation, a wiki, or, in one case, a flash animation, again leveraging and building on the work they had done throughout the year and students' interests and talents.

Culminating into → select from familiar option

Bringing Together Research and Practice

Reading the AL Brief, Brice emphasized that the root of his work came in helping students to develop confidence in their writing and roles as readers and writers. He explained, "This document tells me what I see each day. Kids need confidence in order to engage, and they have to engage in order to grow. That is one part of why we work to build a strong community in school and in class. We learn alongside one another." This community begins with the construction of "caring, responsive classroom environments [which] enable students to take ownership of literacy activities and counteract negative emotions that lead to a lack of motivation" (4). Further, Brice emphasized that though it might appear simple, one of the hardest parts of his work is in "playing with the social nature of literacy enough to get kids to buy in and start growing community" (2). Here, technology served as a tool to bring students together or facilitate the work of the group.

Brice argued that reading the brief also poked additional holes in what he'd seen as a unit that had some successes and, yet, areas that he wanted "to go back and do right." As much structure as he had built into the unit, there were still multiple points where students were confused or unsure about what to do. He explained, "A screencast of how to embed a comment in Google Documents isn't as useful as a screencast of a writer reading and responding to a piece of writing within Google Documents. Students needed the latter, and I only saw it on the other side." As the brief argues, "Student-chosen tasks must be supported with appropriate instructional support or scaffolding" (4).

The brief also worked to affirm Brice's thinking about the "invitation" posed to student writers (and readers) when he presented the option of writing through images, sound, digital narrative, etc. He read, "If they are not engaged, adolescents with strong literacy skills may choose not to read and write (4)," and emphasized, "I have smart writers and yet when I say that there is only one way to be creative and present your work, I close off that part of them that I really want to engage." In other words, working with multimodal texts provided his students with another way to demonstrate how they were smart, and he leveraged that to help them see that they were smart writers.

Ed: Not Born Digital, Learning to Live (and Teach) Digitally

Ed has been teaching at Burns High School for fourteen years, with assignments ranging from grades 9–12 and AP to assistive learning as well as work with the debate team. Burns High is an older building that recently has been rewired to support high-speed access in most classrooms. Ed has three computers in a "writing center" at the rear of his classroom and a laptop and projector at the front of the room for teacher use and presentations. This year he is teaching eleventh-grade honors and on-level classes following a semester block schedule. He explains (with a huge laugh), "It often feels like cartoon English as we move so quickly to pack what I might have done before in over a year into a semester. So the cartoon part comes when I think about the giant Acme hammer that is due to crash on us at any second."

The Tools at Hand

When we talked about the tools he used when planning and implementing instruction, Ed's comments were firmly planted in thinking about how he worked alongside his students. He shared, "Okay, so if I'm being completely open, I'm drawn to think about new literacies and technology because I'm struggling to stay relevant. I recognize what I don't know, and, by sitting next to a kid in the class and saying 'show me,' he gets that I see him and that we can learn together." Over the course of the past academic year, he has learned how to use Flickr, iMovie, the list of podcasts available on the NPR website, and a handful of online tools, such as Wordle, by listening to students and opening up his curriculum enough "that they can present what they know and are learning and are writing through whatever tool or means best fits their work. I learn. And they teach one another. It's never even, but I try to support learning across the whole class." He admitted that these might be tools that others have already discovered and used but explained, "If it is something that lets me work and think in new ways, I don't care how long it has been out. New to me is enough."

[margin handwritten note: personal growth, not just latest, cutting edge]

He also spoke of his disposition as a teacher as a kind of tool at his disposal when it comes to "recasting" his teaching or flexibly thinking alongside new practices and needs. He explained, "Just as I get giddy . . . don't poke fun at that. . . . When new books come into the book room, I get really excited whenever I learn something new that can work in my classroom. I teach because I want to show kids what that means." Ed's classroom can easily be described as literacy-rich—every available space is filled with a bookshelf lined with paperbacks; bright posters with guiding questions and prompts meant to stimulate active reading line the walls; and learning centers surround the room that feature what he calls "language play," holding linguistic games, grammatically error-rich newspaper or magazine articles, crossword puzzles, or audio books. He offered, "Kids can't call themselves readers or writers unless they are doing it. And my classroom is my place for doing it with them."

In the Classroom

As many steps as Ed took this year to meaningfully bring new literacies practices and Web 2.0 tools into his classroom teaching (including but not limited to maintaining a class blog, using podcasts to support students' work as readers and writers, and using gabcast.com for students to share book reviews with one another), his most striking use of technology was tied to supporting his own learning. He offered, "I read blogs of teachers and technology support folks, and I keep my own blog which I use to hold new ideas and links. That's the best PD I get." His learning is also fueled by audio texts: "I listen to NPR podcasts like a junkie. And I just found a new one called 'Conference Connections' which holds all kinds of presentations by teachers and thinkers at Ed Tech conferences. Smart folks."

[margin handwritten note: Blogs, Nings (ECN) as PD — has been very beneficial for me as well]

The learning resource that moved Ed the most was a Ning community that a student teacher in his department shared. He explained, "I'm sitting in the department office, reading Teri Lesesne's latest book, when along comes a student teacher working with one of my colleagues. She saw what I was reading, nodded, and said, 'Yeah, I know her work. I talked to her last night.'" She took Ed to the computer and showed him the English Companion Ning, set up by Jim Burke in early 2009 to support communities of secondary English teachers. Present and participating in the community were the names of teacher-authors that lined his bookshelf of teaching texts. After setting up an account, he quickly found himself reading and responding to discussions about the books he taught, questions about the use of rubrics to assess student writers, and new teachers' questions about negotiating school cultures. Within a few days, he was posting his own questions. He explained, "It was like stepping into the department office that I've always wanted to have here. So, teachers thinking about what they do, and doing the most important thing we do to learn—asking questions. I learn every time I go in there."

As much as Ed learned about different media and tools from his students, he had specific goals for what he wanted them to learn from him about those same spaces and texts. He explained, "So, they are surrounded by so much, but I'm not convinced that they know how to wade through it, how to discern what is rich and useful, and how to use it to do anything." He valued transparency in regularly modeling how new media and emerging tools impacted his own reading, writing, and teaching. He continually emphasized, "This is what I do with books and print texts. I model what a smart reader does, and I try to do it out loud so they see the thinking. As much as I scaffold it or build it into assignments, experience tells me that they need to see it, think about it, and do it themselves for it to stick."

Bringing Together Research and Practice

While Ed read the AL Brief as a tool for understanding how new literacies practices and emerging tools could and were impacting his teaching, he also read it to understand the ways he was using these tools both to shape and inform his own learning. He first pointed to the idea of the shifting literacy environment outside our classrooms, that "literacy extends to new media" (2) and "adolescents [bring outside experiences in] to develop new literacy resources and participate in multiple discourse communities in and outside of school" (3). A teacher who was concerned with developing the reading and writing skills of *all* kids in his classroom, he saw new literacies practices as openings, explaining, "If I devalue or reduce the importance of what kids are doing to produce and read texts outside of my classroom walls, I ignore what they can do, and I limit what we can do together."

Ed identified the importance of developing students' confidence as readers and writers, but he also spoke to developing his own confidence. He explained, "When kids talk about the spaces in which they read and write, I can't lock it out because it threatens my own confidence. Instead, it is an opportunity." Literary scholars are engaging with multimodal texts that require new practices of readers and writers, work that changes the landscape of our field. Ed spoke to the importance of helping students gain access to multiple literacies and the dominant ideas in our field because "learning the literacies of a given discipline can help adolescents negotiate multiple, complex discourses and recognize that texts can mean different things in different contexts" (3). He offered, "That is supposed to be my area of expertise. I have to keep learning in order to do that well and if what we do in our class is going to really matter."

He also emphasized the importance of working as a community, whether that is a community of learners inside the classroom or a community of teachers looking to better understand their practice and how to engage students in meaningful ways. According to Ed, "When I talk within a community that hears and values what I'm trying to do, it challenges me to reach a little. The community responds, and I reach a little more. They get as much as they give, and we share commitment to kids." Ed's trust of his learning network inspired him to set a goal of posting all of next year's lesson plans in Google Documents in order to receive feedback from an engaged, expert audience, and to, again, be transparent about his practice. Where the brief makes multiple statements about the importance of developing rich classroom environments and communities, it also emphasizes that "instruction should center around learners" (4). Ed shared, "This is it. This is what my learning looks like outside of the classroom. It doesn't make sense if my students' learning is completely locked into a curriculum that sees every kid as the same kid. We build a community where we want divergent skills and perspectives. That is what is real."

Making Meaning across Teachers' Stories

Liz, Brice, and Ed are all teachers whom I'd like to have as colleagues. One reason for that is how each of them challenges me to think in new ways about my pedagogy and the students with whom I work. First and foremost, they remind me of the power of learning together, whether it is alongside our students as Liz did with students' podcasted work or alongside our peers as Ed did within the Ning community. Despite the changes that new media and technologies have opened, when it comes to thinking about what it means to be literate, these are changes that we can best navigate together because "literacy is social" (NCTE 3) and "caring, responsive environments enable [learners] to take ownership of literacy activities" (4). Amidst the flurry of changes, what stays constant is our goal of helping kids to work as self-directed, self-regulated learners who make meaning from and with a range of texts and who know how to share their understanding through those media that are the best fit for their audience and the knowledge they are looking to share. These teachers also celebrate and create spaces for students' expertise in negotiating social networks, locating and using media files, and publishing in different media. And, as in these classrooms, we learn together.

[handwritten margin note: social aspect / students and teachers as learners]

Each of these teachers identified a gap between their strategies and knowledge and students' media and engagement. And they each identified methods for their professional growth that tap into new media and differ from what we typically find in schools. Ed engages in an online community of English teachers. Brice uses social tools (e.g., social bookmarking) and media files (e.g., podcasts) to read and listen in on the thinking of teachers and theorists who are working to critically evaluate and use emerging tools. Web 2.0 tools, such as blogs, social networks, and tools for file and media sharing, are such a part of Liz's daily literacy practices that she has to work to draw them out as specific to Web 2.0 or something "new."

This is a tumultuous time, and one in which it can often be easier to think through a filter that prevents the kinds of rethinking and reinventing that new literacies practices make possible. We can think of ourselves as digital immigrants. We can argue that we have successfully engaged and taught students without new tools or practices, or that we can't access labs and lack technical expertise and support. And, in many cases, we are the only teachers in the building who are doing this kind of genuinely hard work.

Or, we can listen to the voices of our students and colleagues like Liz, Brice, and Ed who see power in engaging within a broader English curriculum, one that brings together traditional practices of reading and writing *and* new literacy practices fostering information literacy, working in online communities, and composing through new modes and media. As Applebee argues:

> It is primarily in English class that students deal with questions of what it means to be human, to be just, to be caring, to be autonomous beings in a larger world. And it is also primarily in English class that they hone the reading, writing, and thinking skills that they need to make their mark in the debates they develop.
>
> In the ideal English class, they will do this by embracing all of the tools and media available to express themselves in our twenty-first-century culture, not just those of the nineteenth and twentieth centuries. (73)

Chapter Four

Information Navigation and Critical Evaluation

Students need to move from being simply knowledgeable to being knowledge-able.

—Michael Wesch

Let's get real. Going online for me is like taking a drink from a fire hydrant.

—Angelo, period four, eleventh-grade on-level English

In the chapters that follow, I explore teacher practice and student learning in classrooms that are specifically working to bring together the multiple literacies adolescents bring into our English classrooms, meaningful new literacies practices, accessible digital tools, and the more traditional literary and language tasks at the core of our discipline. I invite you to continue thinking with me and the teachers and students profiled in these chapters as we consider the ways in which students (whether or not they come to us digitally literate) and teachers (whether they are born digital or living digital lives) work to navigate and leverage new and traditional literacy practices to become more skillful readers and writers. This inquiry will be organized around three

big ideas/areas: reading and composing multimodal texts (in Chapter 5), supporting and fostering collaboration and community through participatory media (in
Chapter 6), and, in this chapter, information literacy.

Why begin with information literacy? As teachers (and users of online
technology), we know that navigating the surge of information found online has
become so much harder. We read about the avalanche of texts, pages, and media
available online from a dizzying range of diverse sources. Having that information
where and when you want it is a literacy in and of itself. Today, for example, as I
walked to campus, I listened to a podcast of a lecture delivered by Michael Wesch
at the 2009 Educause Learning Initiative Conference. He is one of those thinkers who makes me squirm, both because of how smart he is and how he ticks off
statistics about the growth and nature of the Internet that typically leave me excited
about the opportunities for my students and, in all honesty, more than a little over-
whelmed. According to his talk today:

1. There are more than 1.5 billion online users.

2. The information newly created and posted online today will be the equivalent
   of sixty new books per second.

3. All of that data are literally floating through the air around us.

4. We are rapidly moving toward ubiquitous information, available everywhere,
   and at unlimited speed (Wesch).

This is the information landscape now—and in the not-so-distant future. As much
as I worry about which of my students are struggling to even get access to the
technology allowing them to "tap" this stream of information, my bigger concern
comes when I think about how to help students leverage that same stream in smart,
intentional ways that advance their thinking. Bottom line—this is hard work.

When my more information literate, digitally savvy students toss out terms
like *pipes*, *feeds*, and *tags*, all tools for how they harness and narrow the information
coming at them, I often feel lapped. That said, despite the ease with which they
toss around terms signaling a different kind of information literacy, when I walk
into the lab and carefully watch all of my students work online, the majority still
move from screen to screen, unable to filter between the sites and information they
want and can use and those that won't push or lead their thinking further. These
are often the kids whom I see follow tangents, lose significant "chunks" of time
(sometimes without even realizing it), and end up satisfied with following only the
first two or three links found when conducting a Google search.

Looking across my students (and all of those for whom the extremes I've just
mentioned don't capture or represent), a particular set of information literacy skills
jumps to the front of my thinking. In working online, students must locate/gather,
question/critique, connect, and synthesize. As Leu et al. describe, this is a process

of "identifying important problems, locating information, analyzing usefulness, synthesizing information to solve problems, and communicating the solution of others" (4). As English teachers (and readers), this process is familiar to us. These are the steps that smart readers take when working with any print text. What makes the work so complex now, though, is that amidst the volume of online information that is increasingly multimodal in nature, students are doing more. And when they get thrown attempting to find what they need, their work stops or, at the very least, it stops working (Leu et al., "Toward"). Add to this that printing out sources is no longer an effective strategy for managing, collecting, and even annotating the volume of texts found online, and it becomes really apparent just how different and complex the information landscape is becoming.

While the AL Brief does not directly call our attention to the demands of media-rich information literacy, it does emphasize the importance of valuing and integrating into our practice a definition of literacy that "encompasses reading, writing, and a variety of social and intellectual practices that call upon the voice as well as the eye and hand. It also extends to new media" (2). Research supports the reality that students turn to the Internet as their primary research tool (Pew Internet Group n. pag.). That said, students' work in finding, vetting, managing, and using information (including multimodal texts, a variety of media, etc.) is likely a part of what the AL Brief refers to as the literacies that are "largely invisible in the classroom" (2). As we'll explore throughout this chapter, there are multiple instances in the brief that position multimodal literacies and "real-world" literacies in ways that fit cleanly and importantly into our thinking about information literacy in our English classrooms.

Connections to NCTE's Adolescent Literacy Brief

Information Literacy Is . . .

- **A "real world" practice**

  "Engagement is encouraged through meaningful connections." (4)

  "Providing student choice and responsive classroom environments with connections to 'real life' experiences helps adolescents build confidence and stay engaged." (4)

- **Multimodal**

  "Literacy encompasses reading, writing, and a variety of social and intellectual practices that call upon the voice as well as the eye and hand. It also extends to new media—including nondigitized multimedia, digitized multimedia, and hypertext or hypermedia." (2)

  "When students are not recognized for bringing valuable, multiple-literacy practices to school, they can become resistant to school-based literacy." (2)

- **Driven by students' inquiry**

  "Instruction should center around learners. Active, inquiry-based activities engage [all] readers and writers." (4)

  "For teachers . . . teaching with approaches that foster critical thinking, questioning, student decision-making, and independent learning." (6)

- **Collaborative**

  "Adolescents need bridges between everyday literacy practices and classroom communities, including online non-book-based communities." (4)

  "[Students] regularly use literacies for social and political purposes as they create meanings and participate in shaping their immediate environments." (3)

Pairing this charge with the realities that Leu and Wesch describe leads me to see the role of the English classroom in fostering information literacy as work that empowers all of my students to think critically about how they access and consume media (including print texts—not just those found through keystrokes) and what they do to keep hold of what they find/value and communicate what they understand. In other words, we work alongside our student readers and writers in knowing how to find, manage, critically unpack, and use the texts that we find online.

Within this chapter, I explore one teacher's methods for changing the way we think about and teach information literacy practices embedded within a ninth-grade I-search unit. Or, following Angelo's insights at the start of this chapter, I examine how one teacher worked to help her students drink from the hydrant and meaningfully use what they find. I do so by taking apart some key instances of instructional practice and thinking, examining what students did (and did not) learn and create, and reflecting on the challenges and questions that this work continues to present.

From a Teacher's Point of View: Considering Information Literacy

Erin has been teaching ninth-grade English at Cooper High School for six years, working across multiple sections of honors, on-level, and reading-support classes. In an attempt to support students during their transition into the high school, the ninth grade functions as a grade-level team, working to collectively support students and developing/implementing two interdisciplinary units across the academic year. Within the English curriculum, students are required to do multiple pieces of writing, all of which are tied to a continually developing electronic portfolio. By the start of the second term, students across all "levels" have written literary analyses, personal narratives, reviews, a persuasive essay, and an I-search paper.

In terms of technology access, the ninth-grade team has dedicated access to both two laptop carts (holding a minimum of twenty MacBooks) and a small lab space in the library/media center. Three labs across the school are also made available to classes that sign up, a process that needs to begin several months in advance in order to secure access during the windows of time in which a unit will run. Though the school network is tied to a restrictive set of filters, teachers are encouraged to submit a written application to the building's technology support staff to petition for opening access to a specific website for students' academic uses. Further, Erin's assistant principal has been a strong advocate, helping her to make the case to "open" those sites that she needs and to help showcase students' resulting work and growth.

Starting Points: A Framework for Thinking about Pedagogy

As a classroom teacher (and even in many instances now as a teacher educator), I followed the same sequence of steps as I prepared to teach a unit: reading and re-reading any criteria/guidelines as outlined in the curriculum or standards guide, examining the sample student work I'd held onto from previous classes (the good, the bad, and the ugly), and delving into my teaching journal entries where I had written about what worked and what "needed help" (my gentler way of saying what bombed). While doing so, I generated a list, ranked in order of what needed the least to the most attention and triage:

1. I am doing _____ well but can do better.
2. What watching my students' literacy practices teaches me that I want to build upon: _____ .
3. _____ isn't working.

This process and series of three-question stems has grown into a standard procedure/protocol that I now use when I work alongside teachers in the field to prompt our mutual thinking about how to open up and revise any instructional task, especially those involving new literacies and emerging tools.

As we'll discuss in the pages to follow, I was surprised that Erin's teaching about Internet fluency and research skills was *not* tied to her work in the I-search unit. The I-search assignment requires students to conduct original research, exploring a self-identified, self-selected topic emerging from a topic list recorded in students' notebooks while completing current events readings across the previous grading periods. Most of the instructional time dedicated to the project (approximately six weeks) is used for a combination of student writing time, mini-lessons in response to how students work in developing their papers, and peer review. While the outcome is a seven- to eight-page research paper, the I-search paper model used in this unit encourages students to write in the first person, to write about their reading and thinking processes alongside their findings, and to work with a variety of sources and resources to support their work.

When we met at the start of the semester to identify lessons and days she'd like me to observe, Erin spoke about Internet fluency as "a set of skills that cannot be limited to a unit or a specific paper. Students need to know what tools to use to find answers to their questions, not just how to research within a framework of a paper assignment." The lessons she and I unpack here all come at the start of the first semester, given her instructional goal that this practice (and the resulting "lens" that students develop when it comes to investigating online information and resources for locating that information) inform students' work any time they were going online to find specific information. To Erin, "This isn't just about English class, though it is a part of my standards. This is one of the bigger life skills that I can help students to develop."

As much as Erin identified the positioning of these activities in the overall scope and sequence of her teaching as a strength, she also spoke of her own skills in locating information as an asset. She offered, "I know I'm doing a good job of exposing students to a range of search engines and tools. I share the ones that I actually use, which certainly gives us lots to talk about, but it also helps them to think about how information is presented or how choice of tool or site can impact findings." Erin works alongside the library-media specialist when planning these lessons, both to leverage their collective information and to establish connections for her students. She explains, "I think students need to see us working this out together. They need to know that we're all making new discoveries, and that two people can bring new perspective and strategies to a problem."

Her thinking about community and how students could work together to locate and evaluate information led Erin to respond to the second question stem, identifying students' collaborative work as an area she wanted to build upon. She believed that outside of the classroom her students were working to share, vet, and collaborate around tools and information in ways that were more authentic and useful than what happened inside of the classroom. According to recent research, adolescents who are savvy at searching go through a three-step process: first, "grazing" across multiple information sources to gain understanding; second, a "deep dive" in which the reader delves into findings to read more closely and to begin to analyze information; and, third, engaging in a "feedback loop" by sharing useful links, ideas, and content within a trusted community (e.g., a group of friends in Facebook or a community within Twitter) or "talking back" through a blog or vlog post (Palfrey n. pag.). Erin wanted to tap into this last stage of their work, sharing that "I want to be more authentic and use that feedback loop to bring us together in thinking about learning, searching, and content."

Dealing with the third question stem (_____ isn't working) was difficult for Erin because it meant tackling a challenge that we're all wrestling with as the volume of information available online continues to grow at an exponential rate and the standards we're expected to teach to seem to become increasingly narrow. She explained, "The curricular guidelines and standards tell me that students need to locate and use information that comes from digital sources. I know that we're doing that. But I don't think that my students can tell you much about their strategies or thinking." Erin was pushing here to do something that I continue to struggle with each time I work with kids who look really busy when in front of the computer but who, when asked, can't tell me about their strategies for finding information or selecting specific sources; students who don't take notes beyond writing a clumsy URL when they read; students who stick solely to material they

3 step searching process

find on websites without intentionally considering the merits of other texts; students who celebrate having the stack of printouts in hand but don't have the first clue what to do with them; or students who follow a tangent (sometimes closely linked to the topic, but often not) when searching and watch an entire class period evaporate (Kajder, "Reading Online"; Kajder, "Tech-Savvy"). Our students are busy when they sit down in front of a computer. As Erin realized, "Having the outward behaviors of looking like you know what you're doing isn't enough. I need students to be able to articulate their thinking and choices in the same ways that we work to take apart that work and thinking when they are working with print text."

Matching Pedagogies with New Tools: Conducting Online Research

Demystifying Search Engines

To begin to address her observations and goals during our discussion, Erin moved students through activities designed to develop students' thinking about how they located, made meaning from, and used information that they found online. She situated the work within their discussions about what it means to be a good writer, sharing that "good writers are writing to seek. You're working to figure something out. To do that, you need to ask your own questions and be able to find resources that you can actually use." At the same time, she also acknowledged that this wasn't just about school, that students were working to find information with a variety of digital tools at their fingertips, offering, "I know that you're looking up facts in Google on your iPhone. Our goal is to do that better, too."

For the first activity, she wanted students to use a variety of search tools, actively exploring online content, analyzing the kinds of findings that specific tools were able to generate, and articulating and unpacking their ideas and process as they worked. The most significant challenge in Erin's planning wasn't to develop an engaging framework within which she could encourage students' talk around search tools; it was in figuring out the sites and tools that would be most ripe for discussion. She started with a list of sites she used most regularly and worked with the school library/media specialist to add (and learn about) additional resources. Last, she'd turned to some options students had listed on an area of their interactive classroom bulletin board. On an easel pad that she'd tacked to the wall, Erin had posted the question, "What search tools do you most like to use?" While students had listed Google and Wikipedia (adorning each with underlines, doodles, and graffiti indicating the "importance" of each), she also found sites which searched blogs, podcasts, and other digital media.

As students entered the classroom on the day of the activity, they each selected a 3×5 card listing one of the six Web search tools that they'd explore that day:

Google (www.google.com), Kartoo (www.kartoo.com), FlickrStorm (http://www.zoo-m.com/flickr-storm/), Keotag (http://www.keotag.com/), Similicio.us (http://www.similicio.us/), and Podscope (http://www.podscope.com). In small groups (the composition of which was dictated by which card students drew), students were asked to work together to investigate the site, identify how it worked, try running different searches using keywords listed on the board (e.g., Shakespeare, Cooper High School, commas), and be ready to report back to the class by sharing their findings. Each team was provided with twenty minutes to work and prepare, and Erin circulated from group to group, asking questions, monitoring for understanding, and providing encouragement and feedback where appropriate.

Erin was surprised that, with the exception of Google, these sites were "new" for the majority of her students. She explained, "They put on that they know so much more than they do. Or, I assume that they know more. Regardless, we were all doing some real learning here." After assigning a student scribe who worked to record class notes on the board, Erin led each group through the mini-presentation of each site/tool, including the capacities students had found limiting or intriguing, what findings had resulted, how those findings were presented, and whether students would use that site as a resource. When pushed by the students (and this happened in each class), Erin spoke to her motivation for choosing these sites. In each case, she began by talking about her own uses, speaking to the need to identify a landmark when out with friends the weekend before or the need to find a teaching strategy that might make their study of *Romeo and Juliet* more compelling. She also spoke of the importance of being able to access a variety of media, "as I'm not sure that I can find what I'm looking for if I limit myself to one mode. Sometimes, I find an answer only when I open to images, or to sound. There can be truth there, too."

Using the common keywords allowed the class to look across the sets of findings as another metric for considering how and when a site or tool would be useful to support their work. Students weighed the importance of a site that brought together findings across multiple media (e.g., Google or Keotag) and what purposes they might have for using a site such as Podscope, which searches the content of audio files. Erin described this part of the lesson as "active and noisy as students had some strong opinions, and many kept referencing other sites. I had to pull them in but liked seeing their confidence and ownership. . . . "

The second stage of the lesson asked students to vet some of the results of the common searches, opening the class to a discussion of how they determined whether information was accurate, useful, etc. After asking students to write some ideas/steps in their writer's notebooks, Erin asked them to share their strategies aloud, reflecting later that "in doing so, I wanted them to either identify the thinking that they were using, or to identify, as happened more regularly than not, that they weren't doing much thinking . . . that they were clicking in place of that." She shared a rubric that I'd developed to support my classroom practice, explaining to students that it was a model they'd work throughout the year to edit, change, and fit the kinds of work that they would encounter when searching for information, again both in and outside of school (see Table 4.1). She explained, "If this is to be a useful tool, it needs to matter to your work inside and outside of English. It needs to also be something that becomes a part of your thinking, so the paper moves into your practice. We'll get there."

Examining Practice

We debriefed at the close of the day's instruction, both while the events of the day were fresh and when Erin was ready to plan where to head next. She explained, "As much as I plan, after I see what happens in the classroom, it all moves around again." She was excited by the volume of discussion that had marked the day, and was encouraged that she'd, at the very least, exposed her students to tools that went beyond what they typically thought to use. She offered, "It's always Google, Google, Google. . . . But I wanted to get outside of that because we need to understand why we go there and make it a choice rather than reflex." Students had surprised her with the ways in which they located and evaluated information. She explained, "Students perpetually ask 'why are we doing this?' That happened today, but it was a question about possibility. . . . Our discussions were signaling that their search process mattered, and that our class is a place for pursuing your own questions."

Her thinking kept returning her to comments made by Royce, a student in her lively second-period class. As his group shared their thoughts on the relative merits of using Kartoo.com to support their search, he'd articulated what was essentially a think-aloud, voicing what he'd thought as he read the screen, navigated the options within the search window, and considered how the findings were presented. "What he did was what I want all of my students to do," Erin shared. "He moved through that page with intent, pausing to question and think, connecting to other texts when he could, and doing his best to evaluate." She identified this as an area she needed to build on: "I set it as a goal for all of my students to do this when they work with literature. I teach them a scaffold for it because it is hard and . . . invisible. Reading online is like that, too." The more she considered a think-aloud protocol to support students' online reading, the more potential she saw in using those moments to provide feedback through formative assessment. She offered, "Luckily, it is early enough in the year that I have time to develop that, and I can't do that without involving [my students] as my insights come from watching and listening to them work."

Table 4.1: Scoring Rubric for Evaluating Reliability and Credibility of Webpages

Criteria	No Information	Some Information	Rich and Relevant Information
1. Determine the author's expertise on the topic.			Information includes the author's occupation, experience, and educational background. This is found within the site, not just on the target page.
2. Learn more about the site where the page appears.			Information includes who supports the site (an individual's page, an educational site, an organization, a commercial site) and contact information.
3. Check out the links from the author's page to other webpages.			The facts/pictures/videos can be substantiated at other sites. Links add to both credibility and resources available. External links are to helpful sites.
4. Find out which webpages have links pointing to the author's page or to the sponsoring organization's site.			Information from sites that link to the author's page is legitimate and provides documentation for the author's page.
5. Look for "pages on the Web" rather than webpages about the author or the organization.			Information is triangulated (available from at least three sources) and uses traditional as well as online resources.
6. Determine how recently the page was published or updated.			Information is included about the date of publication. The date is timely, especially in relation to the content.
7. Assess the accuracy of the information in the document.			Information is included about the accuracy of the content and its presentation.
8. Look for bias in the presentation of the webpage.			Information includes an examination of language in the site.
9. Assess the evidence presented to support opinions or conclusions expressed in the document.			Information includes evidence to support opinions and conclusions expressed in the pages.
10. Check to make sure that the information included is complete and, if applicable, cited from a current source.			Information is not "under construction." Copyrighted material is cited and an effort to maintain timeliness is reflected.
11. Check whether design of the site promotes the information and reflects balanced use of "bells and whistles."			Multimedia, if any, assist in conveying information AND are appropriate.

From The Tech-Savvy English Classroom *by Sara Kajder, Portland, ME: Stenhouse Publishers, 2003.*

Returning to her list of three goals for this instructional sequence, Erin directed her attention to her next step. "We are still early in establishing class community, but I want to again start with students' information-locating skills and then layer on skills that help them to think about what they find. I want them to take what they find and talk back . . . together." While the website evaluation rubric could be a part of that work, she was quick to emphasize that it was meant to be a scaffold and not a constant, explaining, "We can use that to prompt response but there will be a time where I take it away and expect students to be there. After all, no one has ever handed me a rubric when finding, evaluating, and using information outside of school." And so, while the next day's activity would require students to use the rubric as a tool for evaluating content that their online searching would yield, she was more focused on the ways that their thinking about and discourse around that text would provide a deeper, more authentic means of evaluation.

Matching Pedagogies with New Tools: Using Resources, Supporting Thinking

After students had spent one ninety-minute instructional period on the previous work of evaluating a variety of search tools, discussing their own strategies for locating and evaluating online information, and using a rubric designed to help focus their evaluation skills, the next lesson was focused on developing students' skills in identifying, bookmarking, and discussing/evaluating/using the information they found. Erin had rearranged the desks in the room to face together in groups of four or five. Though students were eager to tear into the laptop cart at the front of the room, Erin wanted them to first be working with their print-based readers/ writers notebook and left unpacking the cart for later (much to her students' visible dismay).

Opening their notebooks, students were asked to freewrite about their strategies for organizing, saving, or "holding onto" information found online. After approximately five minutes, she asked each team to share their ideas with one another and identify one strategy that needed to be shared with the fuller class community. The resulting discussion revealed that students had a lot in common across their work, revealing that they most regularly printed websites, copied text that was saved into a word processor, or emailed it to themselves, creating a folder in their email account that held their materials. Erin affirmed each of these, slowly sat back, and sighed, "That is what I used to do, too." She shared an anecdote about her master's thesis, describing reams of paper that she'd printed, and the links she'd bookmarked across multiple computers. "Do you want to see how I learned to do this better?"

Erin used the projector to display contents from a Diigo account that she'd used with peers in a graduate class. She explained that Diigo (which stands for Digest of Internet Information, Groups, and Other Stuff) was a social bookmarking site that allows her to do the following things with the information she finds when searching:

1. **Bookmark the site**
   (i.e., allows access to every bookmark you save to your Diigo account by logging into your account from any computer.)
2. **Highlight information on the page**
   (i.e., leaves a "markup" that appears on that page when you view it through Diigo.)
3. **Add a "sticky note"** (i.e., allows you to comment on each page.)
4. **Save bookmarks by tagging**
   (i.e., allows you to create your own virtual index across all the bookmarks you save with this tag.)

Erin's students were abuzz. In several other content areas, conducting collaborative research was a staple assignment. She had yet to share the social and collaborative aspects of what Diigo allows, and yet students already were visibly excited about the ways this site would help in organizing their work in and outside of the English classroom.

In preparing for the lesson, Erin already had created a group for the class and accounts for each of her students. Diigo offers educator accounts that allow for the speedy (and safe) creation of student accounts (which do not require an email address) and that are limited to participating within the network of their classmates and their teachers. Student accounts are not public, nor can students be found in the People Search index on the Diigo website. Erin reflected, "Your account is private here because it doesn't have to be more. This is about our place for learning together as a class. We'll have lots of other opportunities for more. Just not within here." Participating within a group adds a collaborative aspect to bookmarking and note-taking as content shared to the group is visible to all of its members, allowing for continued discussion across notes and highlights.

What followed was a tightly designed lesson, giving students the room they needed to explore a new site and supporting them in successfully contributing to and completing the assigned task. To respond to any technical glitches, Erin had worked with a team of students during the last week's lunch periods, showing them the class Diigo sites and ensuring that she'd have support in case other students in the class ran into trouble during the lesson. She explained, "It really isn't a difficult technology to use, but I want to be sure to work from the knowledge of many as opposed to trying to be in fifteen places at the same time. As an added bonus, I have come to know my volunteers in important ways."

Before going into their own group space in Diigo, Erin modeled her participation in other Diigo groups for English teachers, in part to demonstrate what students would find, and also to help generate some rules to guide how the class community would run. She explained that this was a site that was meant to be an ongoing resource, "so, working in Diigo won't be like coming into a space, creating something, and forgetting about it. This is almost like a different kind of textbook, and, as we're building it together, it matters." After a healthy class discussion, the list of early rules read:

1. **When adding a bookmark, it must have a tag**.
   (Students valued that everything here needed to be searchable and part of an ongoing discussion.)

2. **Use tags from our class dictionary**.
   (Instead of having hundreds of isolated tags, using a tag dictionary really allows for an index-like organization. Because Erin already had populated the initial dictionary with the names of their major thematic units and a few authors, students could suggest tags that she'd add to the list. The goal here was to keep it concise.)

3. **Be a good citizen**.
   (As students can comment on one another's comments on the pages saved in Diigo, there was lively talk of protecting one another's ideas and that disagreement needed to be "scholarly.")

4. **It needs to be really good.**
   (Students were concerned that it would be too easy to "junk up" the Diigo site with links rather than populating it with well-chosen, specific resources. This was an area that the class agreed to return to soon once they actually started bookmarking sites and adding content.)

Next, Erin shared their task for the class period. Working in small groups, students were to share compelling reading sites and resources on adolescent literature to the class Diigo site. The suggested tags were adolescentlit, reading, and independentreading (a tag tied to the thirty minutes of daily reading that students were expected to complete outside of class). Groups were limited to sharing the best two resources that they found. Fresh from their discussion of the importance of sharing only valuable resources to the class Diigo site, students were encouraged to verbally share across groups before adding a site to the class website. Students each retrieved a laptop from the cart, logged on to the school network, and then were off and searching. Erin circulated throughout the lab, checking in with students and talking with them about the resources they were sharing and discussing. "I was surprised that most of the students went straight to a site they already use and spent their time discussing why we'd want to post it to the class resources. I expected to see more searching and pulling them to talk. We were noisy from the start."

Student groups were given approximately thirty minutes to locate, discuss, and post resources, with most finishing ahead of the deadline and working to either use the sites that were posted (e.g., setting up an account at goodreads.com to create their own virtual library) or comment within Diigo on those sites and resources that their peers had shared. The sites added to the class group ranged from lists of suggested books to sites meant to support communities of readers like LibraryThing.com and BookGlutton.com. Though the close of the period was rapidly approaching, Erin took time to examine a growing set of students' comments around a bookmarked 2005 NPR podcast page that focused on Jon Scieszka's "Guys Read" projects. Ed and Gia, who were working in two different physical groups in the class, were engaged in a discussion on a "sticky note," talking about what makes a story appeal to a guy reader rather than a girl. At one point in the note, Ed explained, "I don't just want to read things that are meant to appeal to my 'guy side.'" Although the class had not yet discussed or formally explored the social functions of the site, they'd already started to use the tools in Diigo to mark up and talk about the content they'd found. Erin commended that, affirming that there was much there for them to discuss both about the site that had struck their interest and the potential of using Diigo to comment collaboratively on sites, and she connected some of their ideas to an upcoming independent reading project using dialogue journals. Gia shared, "That's why I'd want to put something here. I want you all to see it, but I'd rather we talk about it, too. That's the point, right?"

Apart from assigning reading for the next week and reminding students about the proper way to return their laptops to the cart, Erin's closing remarks helped connect what students had done during this day to the work ahead, but, more important, they provided context for looking at what they had done. "We're just at the earliest point of using Diigo as readers and writers. We have so much to talk about, but I want to remind you that we own this site collectively—as a group. It is another learning space."

Examining Practice

These were early lessons, each meant to start a conversation with students about research and information fluency that would be continued throughout the school year. In doing so, Erin exposed them to a tool set that acknowledged multimodal content, that encouraged participation, and that affirmed that research is about pursuing answers to questions that we care about. Similar to where she found herself at the close of the first lesson, Erin's thinking was focused on what she could learn from what happened during the day, and how that could inform her practice in later lessons.

Her thinking first focused on the students' response to Diigo. She explained, "I want to use Diigo with students because of how it changed my own thinking about research. I started us by just looking at the bookmarking and annotating part. I didn't expect they'd see the collaboration yet." She turned to Gia and Ed's discussion as support for her thinking that her students would benefit from opportunities to not only find and discuss sources but also to engage in conversation that was on the very page. She offered, "This isn't pressing print. It also isn't formal. I can ask students to write differently here because it is discussion. They can try out an idea. Feedback comes from more than me."

Though she had yet to really think about how she'd assess/evaluate student participation in Diigo, she was adamant in valuing the work that she saw students doing as they bookmarked, annotated, and commented on texts. She explained, "My students will be present in a new way here. They select part of the content. They respond and question. This is a different classroom, even though I've done much on my end to keep it safe." Erin is an avid reader, and each of our discussions was full of references to what she'd read in the newspaper or other media sources about students' digital identities. She voiced real concerns that students were creating a footprint that focused on creating social personas and looked to their work in Diigo as a different kind of opportunity. Erin offered, "I might be reaching too far here, but this is a part of creating a digital identity that reflects how my students work as readers and writers. This is how I want them to be known."

She voiced specific goals for later work, all of which remained rooted in developing students' collaborative skills (her third instructional goal for this work). She explained, "I want to start small, build intentional activities that lead students to work in Diigo, and, when we're ready, I want to collaborate with students outside of our classroom. That's real-world work for what we can do there." Trusting the security provided by setting up class and student accounts through her educator account in Diigo, Erin identified that the work would reach a different level of authenticity and insight when students would post and discuss resources with other classes (again, all of whom would work within the private, education-specific side of Diigo). However, she felt that getting her students to that point would take time, sharing, "This isn't a this-semester goal, and it might not even be a this-year goal. I have a lot of thinking and learning to do. Lucky though . . . I get to think it through alongside my students."

On the Horizon

For some, a Google search is the oxygen of their daily life in the information world.

—Clay Shirky

There is something in the air, and it is nothing less than the digital artifacts of over one billion people and computers networked together collectively, producing over 2,000 gigabytes of new information per second.

—Michael Wesch

Many ideas in this chapter are not new as tasks or concepts in our work in the English classroom. Research writing has evolved into a "staple assignment" across grade levels, presenting students with opportunities to engage in a process of identifying, vetting, and synthesizing texts which aid in complicating, challenging, supporting, and growing their ideas and argument. What has changed, and rather dramatically, is the ubiquity of information we now can access by keystroke, and, I'd argue, more important, the work of that search. When I first started teaching, I worked alongside our librarian to help students start by first understanding where they were going to look and then what they'd be looking to find. Searching online reverses the order of that process.

To prepare students to locate, critically evaluate, and use information (a goal that I'd argue is of prime interest in the English classroom), we have to change what we're doing. We have to figure out how to best work within a process that hinges around a means of seeing what comes up, and doing so in a way that addresses both a digital divide (i.e., access to equipment) and a participation divide (i.e., knowing what tools to use, doing the work, and, in many cases, working within a shared community of practice). It is no longer enough for students to leave our classrooms literate in the practice of locating and vetting print sources only.

Ironically, the heading for this section, "On the Horizon," points us to think about something that is forthcoming—but the topic of information literacy and media literacy is already here. While the Internet on the horizon will likely be marked by more information, more participatory media, and newer and more diverse systems for tagging/making meaning across content (Wesch, "Vision"), access and literacy here is about power. We need to know what the filters are in place that are limiting the flow of information we are able to access in any given context. We need to know how to locate and vet digital information, but we need also to pay particular attention to skills that allow us to critically consider the information environment as it continues to change. Participation will require knowledge, melding those out-of-school literacies that some students bring into our classroom spaces and the critical literacy practices English teachers can bring to bear on that work.

The AL Brief doesn't provide us with a bulleted list of information literacies that need to play a role in how we prepare adolescent readers and writers to work with digital texts. It does something more important, especially as new literacies

[handwritten margin note: important ELA goal]

are developing so rapidly that the list would immediately be dated and narrow. It offers us a broader set of ideas and concepts (e.g., the importance of real-world, inquiry-driven practice; the role of multimodal texts; the participatory nature of genuine collaboration) rooted in Web 2.0/digital literacy practices which have the potential to open up and amplify the work that we do in our English classrooms.

In This Chapter . . .

Website Evaluation and Search Engines

Technologies used:

Google–www.google.com
Flickrstorm–www.flickrstorm.com
Keotag–www.keotag.com
Similicious–www.similicious.com
Podscope–www.podscope.com

Where to go for more information:

- Articles in *Learning and Leading with Technology*, *Edutopia*, and *School Library Journal* that name new and useful sites and tools to consider
- Think U Know–Internet Literacy Site from UK, http://www.thinkuknow.co.uk
- Resources on online searching and information literacy, compiled by Dr. Joyce Valenza (library media specialist and writer for *School Library Journal*), http://informationfluency.wikispaces.com

Using Diigo in the Classroom

Technologies used:

Diigo–http://www.diigo.com

Where to go for more information:

- Creating a Diigo educator account, http://help.diigo.com/Diigo_Educator_Account
- Tutorials by Liz Davis (academic technology director at Belmont Hill School), http://21ctools.wikispaces.com/Diigo

Some tips when working with Diigo:

1. I've been working in several schools that won't allow teachers to download an extension to their browser (e.g., Firefox). Though I find working with Diigo through the browser to be the best approach, there is a small, free application that helps me to access many of those key features: http://www.diigo.com/tools/diigolet.

2. Spend some time talking with students about the ways that they present themselves in Diigo—even when working in an education-only account. In those cases where we want to grow the Diigo community beyond the classes in a specific school, I prefer that students use avatars rather than pictures of themselves. In some cases, we do this by photographing a backpack instead of a student's face. It could also be done using some of the playful comic sites available online (e.g., toondoo.com).

Reading and Writing Multimodal Texts

Chapter Five

> To offer students options is to take a humungous step into the unknown. Not telling students what to write and how to do it goes against the grain of writing teachers who are not writers and readers, but those who write and read feel the necessity of choice. They feel it in their guts.
>
> —Jane Hansen (156)

Situating the Conversation

Leo, a student in first-period eighth-grade English, looked ready to pounce the minute I entered his Monday morning, midway-through-the-semester class-room. He stood in impatient silence as I went about the tasks of setting down a bag and taking out a notebook in order to prepare for that morning's observa-tions. "Good morning, Leo," I offered, grinning at the sight of him, lips clenched as if he were willing his words to stay in his head.

"I can't wait to show you guys this. I've been waiting all weekend! Look! Look!" Leo exhaled, pointing wildly at a clipping from the local newspaper.

After I convinced him that I'd be able to read it better if it were on the desk and not waving madly through the air, I read the title, "Unexpected Twist: Fiction Reading Is Up." "Read it. You'll see. We're not in as much trouble as you English teachers think," Leo announced.

Offering findings from the 2009 National Endowment for the Arts study "Reading on the Rise: A New Chapter in American Literacy," the article celebrated a significant rise in the number of American adults who reported reading literary fiction (e.g., novels, short stories, poems, or plays), from 46.7 percent in 2002 to 50.2 percent in 2008 (Thompson C01). Among other findings, the study identified a rapid increase of literary reading among eighteen- to twenty-four-year-olds, a 21 percent increase that reverses a historically sharp 20 percent decline in the 2002 survey (NEA).

Despite my attempts to point out that the study didn't look at readers in his demographic, Leo sat back in his chair with a smug grin, holding up his copy of *American Born Chinese*, his current choice for independent reading, and nodding in pride. I certainly didn't want to burst his bubble, but my mind immediately leapt to the growing body of literature and statistics that paint a different picture about adolescents' reading.

Some of the statistics are grim. The National Assessment of Educational Progress (NAEP) data from 2007 reveal that only 31 percent of eighth graders are able to read and write with proficiency, with 3 percent performing at advanced levels (Lee, Grigg, and Donahue n. pag.). Here, "proficient" includes skills, such as identifying the genre of a story, recognizing what story action reveals about a character, applying text information to a real-life situation, or recognizing explicit information from a highly detailed article (14). Biancarosa and Snow argue that approximately 70 percent of older readers require some form of remediation to aid in comprehension (16). And the gap between white students' performance and that of our Hispanic and African American students continues to be striking (Lee, Grigg, and Donahue n. pag.).

Like Leo, it is easy for me to get jubilant when we see statistics about an increase in reading. That is a space and a mindset I really want to inhabit. But the reality is that there are very real challenges and opportunities in working with adolescent readers. The work a reader does in comprehending a text is hefty, including but not limited to activating prior knowledge; making connections between and within texts; predicting, inferring, organizing, and holding onto details; revising and modifying your thinking and schema given new information learned while reading; and self-monitoring your own process and work. Students in many of my classes (from my first middle school job to my current graduate class) would be deemed nonreaders by the NEA study and struggling readers given the NAEP 2007 data. That doesn't mean, however, that these students aren't reading; and it doesn't mean that they don't bring really important skills and literacies that we can build on to lead them to greater success and continued motivation.

As I heard Lemke argue in a 2007 speech, as English teachers we are charged with "understanding what is and what is not workable in bringing new literacies into close connection with school learning and traditionally valued literature." As established in earlier chapters, digital youth engage with new media to create, and to read, write, film, document, and represent themselves in a variety of media (Wilber 57). In thinking about the participatory aspects of engagement in social, Web 2.0 spaces, we know that students read to participate in social networks, to develop identity and engage in self-improvement, and to gain information that they can put to use (Moje et al., "Complex"). Reengaging reluctant adolescent readers requires that we create spaces for them to demonstrate the varied ways in which they are richly and flexibly literate. It means that we have to move from "more of the same" (O'Brien 30) to opening up our teaching to include multimodal literacies and practices as points of connection with the traditional curriculum.

Despite his enthusiasm in sharing the article from the *Washington Post*, Leo was one of the lowest performing readers in the first-period class. His test scores were low, and he spoke of reading as "so boring" and "only so that teachers can tell you what you don't know or what you don't pick up from what you were supposed to get." Outside of the classroom, though, he read graphic novels, films, maps, instruction manuals, instant messages, chat room discussions, websites, blogs, wikis, pieces of digital art, and digital narratives/stories. Inside of school, he was seen as a nonreader and an unsuccessful student. Outside of school, he demonstrated a completely different level of confidence and skill, reading a variety of texts across modes, writing through a variety of media, and connecting across texts and media.

The AL Brief urges us to implement an expanded definition of literacy in our classrooms; one that both values and leverages the multiple literacies that Leo brings into our classrooms (see sidebar).

Views inside/outside the school [handwritten marginal note]

Connections to NCTE's Adolescent Literacy Brief

Valuing the Literacies Students Bring into the Classroom

- **Expands our definition of literacy.**
  "Literacy encompasses reading, writing, and a variety of social and intellectual practices that call upon the voice as well as the eye and hand. It also extends to new media—including non-digitized multimedia, digitized multimedia, and hypertext or hypermedia." (2)

- **Allows us to tangibly value the literacies students bring into our classrooms.**
  "The literacies of adolescents are largely invisible in the classroom." (2)

- **Impacts the motivation and engagement of *all* students.**
  "When students are not recognized for bringing valuable, multiple-literacy practices to school, they can become resistant to school-based literacy." (2)

- **Helps create points of connection between out-of-school literacy practices and the more traditional English curriculum.**
  "Adolescents need bridges between everyday literacy practices and classroom communities, including online non-book-based communities." (4)

Within this chapter, I bring these ideas about reading and writing multimodal texts into the classroom as a lens for examining the ways students did (or did not) move as readers and writers, and push the work up against some challenging ideas about literacy that the work opened up. This is what we do as teachers, and it is how documents like the AL Brief are often the most useful, as a lens for re-seeing the energy and motion that mark our work when we learn alongside students.

From a Teacher's Point of View: Building Readers' Confidence and Voice

Kristen teaches eighth grade at Whitman Middle School. At this school that does not formally track students, her classes represent a range of interest levels, talents, and "histories" resulting from former English classes (and teachers), as well as perspectives and experiences given the rich cultural diversity represented across the school. She teaches four sections of eighth-grade English, all within the "Panther" team. All units are thematic in design, allowing for regular instances of interdisciplinary practice. The team is a mix of experienced and relatively new teachers; the most senior member opened the school twenty-two years ago, and the youngest is starting his first year. Kristen has taught for six years, all at Whitman.

Technology access is inconsistent across the school. Resources are allocated to instructional teams based upon required curricular projects and past history (i.e., who has used which tools for what specific tasks). The building has a wireless network, but the majority of computers available are desktops in traditional labs. The firewall is particularly tight, and lifting the lock on specific sites can be a difficult if not impossible task of communicating with building-level and district-level administrators, technology support staff, and, in some instances, curriculum coordinators. Kristen's team successfully advocated to remove a block on Skype last year so they could communicate with experts at the British Museum when teachers wanted to work with resources posted online from an exhibit on portraiture. The site was unblocked for the week of their use and promptly closed back down pending approval for additional uses.

Matching Pedagogies with New Tools: Reinventing the Book Report

All students at Whitman Middle participated in "drop everything and read" (DEAR) independent reading time during each day's morning meeting. Though this was also time that was regularly interrupted for extended announcements or needed team-time, students averaged an hour of reading time a week from this work. Any assessment or "accountability" for students' work rested in the hands of the team English teachers. On some teams, DEAR was a purely recreational activity.

Across the three eighth-grade teams, students composed two- to three-page book reviews for one book per grading period. Students were expected to read both during DEAR time and for twenty minutes each night. Further, as an added incentive, many of the written book reviews were selected by the school media specialist and housed in a "recommendations" binder located in the media center.

In thinking across her goals for this work, and previous experiences with other groups of students, Kristen used the same framework introduced in Chapter 4:

1. I am doing _____ well but can do better.

2. What watching my students' literacy practices teaches me that I want to build upon: _____ .

3. _____ isn't working.

She was quick to emphasize the importance of what she saw as a strength in the work: "I think that we're doing the choice bit well in that kids are bound to choosing a piece of fiction or a work of nonfiction, or in some cases a hypertext fiction or fan fiction, but that depends on the kid." Despite this, she certainly saw cases where this approach was still too narrow a vision. She explained, "I do have some students for whom the work of reading a book is onerous. I'd like to open this up to include audio books, especially as I just found a website, readthewords.com, that could help to generate that." As much as she celebrated that students had a broad range of choices in texts and media, it was a challenge to pair some students with a text that would engage and a format that would empower them—and require that they move outside of their comfort zone.

Beyond the challenges posed by the reading component of DEAR, Kristen looked to ways to challenge the students in the writing component: the book report. Kristen had seen artifacts of her students' multiple literacies emerge in her classes throughout the nine weeks they had worked together and identified that she'd like to leverage their expressive and creative capacities into their classroom work. She explained, "I've seen kids who bring in these detailed, layered graphic novels that they've written, or some who share bits of the music they mix in Garage Band. They are writing all the time. . . . They just don't see it yet." Her sense, at this point, was that if she were to open up the modes through which students could express their understanding, the task of writing would become both more appealing and more rigorous because expression through multiple modes of communication would also raise new possibilities for what students could say about the texts and their reading. She explained, "Composing through image, sound, movement . . . . these are unique in how they communicate, which should result in a different kind of commentary and content from students as they aren't confined to what they can do through print."

Kristen spoke about the third area, "the thing that wasn't working," with the most energy and anticipation. She explained, "Students in my classroom divide up into groups and talk to themselves in discussion. They don't connect with one another, or, better, across one another. We *have* to do that better." Kristen sought to build a class interpretive community that allowed for exchange and negotiation, where students came together rather than splintering off into the groups reflected in the halls outside of the classroom. Most important, she wanted to elevate the level of classroom talk, modeling for all students the ways that discussion could be used to really trigger and move thinking. At this stage of her reflection, she wasn't certain whether community-building would be a result of the use of a specific tool (e.g., text-messaging) or an instructional scaffold built around the practice. "Let me explain," she said. "If I build an experience on my end to facilitate talk, it shouldn't matter the way or space in which that talk happens, right?"

Engaging Student Readers

In support of these observations and goals, Kristen developed a recasting of the book review project, asking students to self-select and read a text (again, of a media of their choosing) and then develop a multimodal response/review that presented their thinking in original images and embedded audio. Students would use Voice-Thread.com as a tool for creating and presenting their work. She explained her selection of VoiceThread as based on her own experience as a user: "I learned about this in Writing Project this summer. It is a simple tool, not as high-end or big as something like iMovie. Students enter images in a sequence and then the tool supports their recording of narration or written comments/feedback." She offered, "I am not going to stand in the front of the room and show students what to do with the technology. My role should be to show them how to use it as a writer. So, it has to be really simple and fluid." To engage class community, Kristen required that students randomly select three peers' projects to comment on as a viewer/participant. The comments could include questions or connections to texts (print or digital) that they'd read or experienced. Further, VoiceThread allowed for the comments to be presented either orally (embedded into the project as an audio file) or as a written response (embedded into the project as a text file).

Where as the independent reading/book review work had never been completed during English class time, this VoiceThread project would. She explained, "I'm not thrilled about it, but at least for this first go, I need to be able to scaffold and support all kids through the work. Some might have it at the start, but most will need to be nudged." She also was slightly unsure about the appeal of the assignment and wanted to provide class time to foster connections and enthusiasm. She explained:

> I want to be sure that they see a point and value to putting more work into this. You can't copy this from the inside cover or rear cover of a book. This requires a whole level of thinking so that some of my kids don't check out before they really start and that others see that this isn't just something they are doing for me.

Students would be provided with two instructional periods of lab time for creating their VoiceThread and one additional period for viewing and responding. As Kristen argued, "First, I have too many kids without computers at home to not do this here. And since they have to go in with a storyboard, a script, or outline, and a ready collection of images, it should move fast." With assistance from the media specialist, Kristen expected all students to come to the task with their original images either scanned or photographed using a digital camera. "To enter the lab," she explained, "students will have preplanned images and gotten them ready to load. So their time will be spent recording what they want to say from their script or an outline and ordering the content." She expected that, if these reviews were successful, the remaining book reviews would also take this multimodal format, and, as students would have already completed one, the amount of class time used would be reduced to a day for composing and a day (or less) for responding.

Kristen was surprised by students' responses when she shared the revisions to the project. She explained, "Apparently, I undervalued my technology knowledge—or I overestimated theirs. They didn't know VoiceThread—and rather liked what I showed them with my own example." Kristen had shared her own multimodal review of a young adult text, *Notes from a Midnight Driver*. To show the full scope of the project, she asked the other four teachers on the team (social studies, math, science, and health/physical education) to respond through audio and written feedback in VoiceThread.

Despite this modeling, preparing for their move into the computer lab was more involved than she'd anticipated. Kristen offered, "I had no idea that they'd be so intimidated or, in some cases, blocked, when it came to thinking about how to visually represent their thinking. And the number of them who were angry that they had to actually create their own images. . . ." While the eventual payoff was high for students who understood that creating your own photograph or piece of art provided an opportunity for doing narrative work through an image, that was a big conceptual leap for students whom Kristen referred to as "print-trained." What changed the tenor of this work was the idea of audience. She explained, "Once kids understood that they were writing for one another, and less for me, they lightened up and were off. . . . It was like the lights came on, or maybe that was a nudge that made this unlike a school project and more like what they want to use tools like this to do."

importance of audience in motivation

As an exemplar, Kristen described what she saw happening in Todd's work (a student in her second-period class). After reading *The Hunger Games*, he shared with Kristen that "[t]his is the first book I've ever been able to really see, and that I've seen myself in as a character—like really see. I'm a little creeped out by that, but I think that is why this project might work." Because he saw the settings in the novel ranging from "scruffy forest to gleaming city," he set out with a digital camera to take pictures of himself and his friends depicting scenes of Katniss in the forest, Petta and Katniss's preparation for the games, and images as they were poised to start the games. His favorite picture was of the back of his friends' heads as they watched a television screen, simulating the viewing of the Hunger Games.

Following his storyboard, Todd uploaded and arranged his images. Once they were set in the right order, he began recording narration that described and unpacked the images and, at times, offered passages from the novel. He explained, "I had to remember that this wasn't a movie. What I was creating was a review that had images, audio, and a little bit of transition to share what I thought about the book. As much as I had to balance not telling too much, I also didn't feel that I had to persuade—just think." Further, Todd's work was unique in that on a few images, he included audio that worked more as a sound track—nature sounds, or a simulated clanking of armor. Here, an image lingered on the screen and was paired with sounds that helped the viewer see what Todd was envisioning as he read. He offered, "I can show you what I see here as opposed to trying to write it. Or, I'm including a quote in a review and assuming you see what I do. That doesn't usually work for me. Now, you see me as a reader in the text. Huh. Hadn't thought like that before. . . ."

Sharing and Evaluating Book Projects

Following the two days in the computer lab (which were tightly managed by Kristen's requirement of the storyboard/image collection "entrance tickets" and her continual countdown of the time remaining before the close of the period), students were set to provide feedback to one another's work. Students' names were placed in a jar in the front of the room. As they entered, students were instructed to select three slips of paper, make sure that their name wasn't in that group, and head to a computer. Once everyone was seated, Kristen asked them to brainstorm the kinds of feedback that would be useful to them in terms of their own work. The list from first period included:

- Reactions to how the pictures matched the spoken words—or didn't
- Questions about the picture, the words, the combination, or the book
- Ideas about other things you've read that might be like this
- What you like in what you are seeing/hearing

To provide feedback or response, students first had to log in to VoiceThread so that responses would be linked to individual students and to the "avatar" or image they selected to represent themselves. Kristen was struck by the importance of that image to most students. "They'll slap an image up in their review, but they'll fret about the avatar image. I guess it represents them in ways that feel closer, but I see the other images as reflecting who they are as readers—which I think is harder."

The format of the feedback, text or spoken, was inviting to students because it provided some flexibility. Kristen explained, "First, I had students for whom print is still an issue. They spoke ideas aloud which seemed to be empowering. Also, length corresponded to mode. When a comment was quick, it was written. When longer, it was spoken." Interestingly, when students had been required to respond to three students' work, several students requested that they be able to do more than that. Kristen took that to be reflective of two things:

> This was a two-layered activity. . . . First part, students had to do the public work of a reader which, for some, was an uncomfortable role. And the second part was all about the social, sharing ideas with readers about their work as readers. Some couldn't do both. Some struggled with the images. But this was the first time I've had everyone participate and do so on time. There's something there for sure.

Audience for the VoiceThread reviews initially was limited to the class, but because each of the projects (once feedback had been secured) could be easily exported/downloaded from VoiceThread, archived projects were shared on computers in the media center, serving as a resource along with the binder of written reviews from other years and, now, other teams.

Let's return to Todd's work. Todd identified the process of receiving feedback as what set this work apart from other writing in the class. The response to his work (by three classmates) was positive. He explained:

> They shared mostly spoken ideas, and they were in two camps. The first batch of comments talked about the images paired with what I read from the text or explained from my head. I got the most from these as when someone talks about you as a reader, it means you were in a good place, right?

Comments that connected his work to other texts (digital and print) weren't as helpful to Todd. "I'm not well-read," he told us. "So, if they talked about something else, I didn't know what that was. I got that they likely made sense, but it didn't help my thinking as I just didn't know what it was." While Kristen was surprised and frustrated that Todd didn't see those comments as an opportunity to drive additional reading, she was excited by another aspect of his work:

> Here is a kid who isn't very vocal in class, and he's talking in really important ways about a book that challenged him. And he's returning multiple times to his

VoiceThread to see what comments he is receiving. Reading, re-reading, and re-reading again. That certainly didn't happen in the print reviews.

Examining Practice

Kristen was pleased with the recasted book reviews, seeing progress in students' reading, writing, and collaboration but also in ways that the project could continue to grow in later uses. "My first goal, to get kids writing in images, went mostly well. I think that we needed some kind of an earlier activity, because for some of my more skilled writers, this was a shift out of what was comfortable and what they already did well." The second mode present in the texts, audio, was an area of unexpected work. She explained:

> I expected to see students write and then record. Instead, I saw them compose as they spoke, and, counter to what I expected, these were better comments than those they'd written. And, like Todd, some kids used audio to illustrate or generate other images. It was a surprise that I'd thought that I'd look at their spoken words in the same way I looked at their writing in the usual way of doing the reviews, and I had to completely change that up as they were doing cool things I didn't foresee.

With the increased range in how students expressed what they knew and how their peers' writing evoked response, Kristen needed to develop a completely new rubric for providing them with feedback and an assessment of their work. She explained:

> I'm really torn about this. I know that they need a grade or some kids won't do it. But I want feedback from me to really move their work as readers. Rubrics feel more final. So I did two things. I didn't want to get into their composition and leave comments, so I stayed out of their VoiceThreads. But I did share my responses with them . . . as a reader . . . paired with a rubric that looked at how they wrote with images and sound, how they used the text to support their work, and how they worked as readers of other students' texts.

Opening up what counts as valued communication requires thinking differently about the ways in which we evaluate and respond to our students' work. As the AL Brief articulates, "Assessment is a means by which students learn and develop," and, here, assessment was as much about capturing where students were as forecasting where they could go next (2).

Kristen's bigger goal of developing community among the students in her classroom did move through this project. With the goal of building on what the brief refers to as a "discourse community," Kristen noted students had made progress "in that commenting in the digital space of VoiceThread increased participation and did more than passing around papers for response." But what she'd hoped would transfer from the VoiceThread into students' interactions in class discussion didn't happen. She reflected, "There are a lot of things here that I need to think about. So this was individual writing for an individual goal that invited feedback to push the individual." To foster collective community, one that was sustained across projects and a part of the culture of the class, the next natural step for Kristen was to move the participation to a more collaborative project. She explained:

> If I want them to be a community and not just peer-to-peer in their responses, I think I'll need a collaborative activity where students start working across groups. This project was about individual identity, and that is where it should be. I need to move next to a task or bigger work that is about a fuller class community.

Matching Pedagogies with New Tools: Developing a Reader's Voice

The second wave of Kristen's exploration of her pedagogy came the next semester, after she'd completed one additional run of the book review/VoiceThread project and firmly knew how she wanted to proceed. Again deploying the three-pronged series of questions meant to push her into thinking about what she was doing well, what she was learning alongside students, and what she wanted to do better, we quickly moved to talking about her new ideas. She celebrated the steps that her students were taking as readers. She explained, "I see a lot of confidence growing in most of my students, and notably for some who are really trying on the voice of a skilled, creative reader for the first time." She spoke with certainty and pride when discussing the ways in which readers were supported and provided with opportunities for choice and voice.

While Kristen's work with the VoiceThread project had helped in moving her classes closer to the interpretive, collaborative community she envisioned, there was still work to be done. Her observations of how digital youth engaged in and outside her classroom centered on their abilities to connect with and work within an online community. Although she'd originally envisioned that she'd tap into this through a collaborative group activity, time observing and talking with kids pushed her in a different direction. She shared, "I don't think that it is as much about groupings as it is working within that group to do something that you care about. So the reason to go online, for our work, would be to grow our community but also to put students' writing to use." She pointed to the brief, reading aloud, "Adolescents are successful when they understand that texts are written in social settings and for social purposes" (3). Kristen explained, "It starts there. I want them writing and thinking socially—not in terms of friends—but in terms of coming together and doing something meaningful. I want that kind of 'always on.'" She wanted to leverage what she was learning about participatory media and multimodal composing to bring together students with differing points of view, experiences, and insights so that they could develop their ideas together.

[handwritten margin note: 3 recurring thoughts / ?s for reflection / to help in mind]

Similar to what happened when we'd talked earlier in the year, Kristen speedily identified the area in her practice that wasn't working: "No matter what I do, it's still for school. I want to make this more than an English class assignment. I want it to be more than that." While she believed this had to do with the imprint of the previous English classes and assignments that students brought into her classroom, she also argued that this could be done by capitalizing on what is important about work inside of the classroom—and what might give it legs outside of the classroom. She explained, "Students are writing and creating content every day. If we were to collect that work and, somehow, transparently get it up online and shared for feedback—and someone's use outside of the classroom—then the relevance should be immediate."

Readers Talk about Their Reading

During the second semester, Kristen used literature circles to support students' discussion, scaffold and explore strategies they deploy when reading, and further develop the "reader's voice" she saw emerging during the first term. Given her goal of building in opportunities for students to engage in new practices and new (at least to her) tools in order to support community and create useful, meaningful artifacts or outcomes, she recast her expectations for the final products required at the close of the literature circles. In the past, she'd invited students to create artistic responses (e.g., a photo essay, a character playlist) that were then shared in a class gallery walk, providing students with an opportunity to return to the book to talk about and support their work. She explained, "As much as students had worked within a group to figure their way through the text, the projects were individual and more of an extension than an outcome."

In reinventing the project for this year's literature circles (in which students would read and work with the novel *Ender's Game*), she told students that instead of the art project/gallery walk final project, each group would create a podcast that would include moments from their discussion and synthesize their response to the book. She explained, "I think it is all present here—so students are all collaborating and all present in the podcast through their voice and their thinking. And I'm asking for higher-order thinking by reflecting on the ways that the discussion worked within that group." As she presented it to students on the first day of the new unit, she shared, "We'll do it as a podcast as I want this to be in your heads outside of the classroom" (motioning to her iPod and earbuds).

And this first-period class pushed back. Students spoke of not "getting it;" once she explained the project for a second and then a third time, they shared what they saw as a misunderstanding about what a podcast is and should do. Hank, a student who worked with three peers to develop the school's sports podcasts (an extracurricular venture of four sports writers on the school newspaper and distributed through the school website and modeled after ESPN's SportsCenter), explained, "If you want a podcast to mean something, you've got to say something in it that is worth listening to. I'm game for this, but I don't want to hear kids' discussions. Don't school-ify this. We can do better." Wanting to explore this discussion more with her students, Kristen began a list on the whiteboard of the qualities that students wanted a podcast developed in an English class but directed toward other readers of a particular text to have. The list included:

1. Content needs to go beyond what is obvious but that still offers help when we're stuck.

2. The podcast needs to work as a resource. Listening would help to answer questions.

3. The podcast needs to include voices outside of our classroom.

4. The podcast needs to receive feedback (rankings, comments, etc.).

Together, Kristen worked with students during that first-period class to shift the podcast assignment into a frame that met students' interests and her own instructional goals. "They had so much energy around this, and they were totally in alignment with the outcomes I wanted to meet. If anything, they did it better, but they understand the genre better than I do."

In the resulting assignment, each literature circle group (approximately five to six students per group) was required to create a podcast (approximately eight minutes in length) at the close of the unit. All students' voices were to be present in the finished product, and, though the requirements had some degree of flexibility to allow for increased creativity, all podcasts needed to include the elements generated in the class brainstorm. To keep it simple and allow herself time to figure out this new task, Kristen decided to do this "enhanced" podcast with only the first-period class, using the gallery walk activity from previous years with other sections. She explained, "There was a lot to think about with this, and I had the resource of a class who was largely doing this alongside me. So it made sense to only grow it once I understood what it was growing out to become. Other students didn't mind—they attributed it to having Hank in the class, and they hoped to use the resulting podcasts as resources."

Building, Evaluating, and Sharing Podcasts

In working alongside students to negotiate curriculum and the project resulting from their work, Kristen was firm about two things. One, she was not willing to give any more time to first period to work on their literature circles and podcasts than she'd originally planned. She explained, "Instructional time is one of the most

negotiate curriculum w/ students, but w/ guidelines

valuable things I have. So we don't have the luxury of going off. Production time had to be the same. Plus, that let me really look at the differences across first and let's say second periods." And she was not willing to teach students how to use the podcasting tools. She explained, "When I'd originally planned this, I'd created some handouts and kept it simpler than this has become. So, again keeping true to the original design, there is about ten minutes to talk about the technology part—and they had to stick to that." Students in the class recommended that they use a combination of Audacity (free audio editing software that works on both Macs and PCs) and gcast.com, a website that could be used to house their podcasts until they figured out a way to connect them to iTunes (which was the students' goal since they were reaching for a wide audience).

In fact, the only tool-centered discussion that occurred in class was raised as students expressed desire for some kind of ranking system that would provide feedback (similar to the points provided in fanfiction or similar sites). As Gcast didn't have that functionality, students created an internal ranking through anonymous feedback submitted using a survey they developed in Zoho Creator and linked to their podcast channel in Gcast. Further, some of the students developed an in-class "box" for paper submissions because they were concerned that listeners in their own school who might not have a computer at home (but could download podcasts onto mp3 players using school or library computers) wouldn't be able to participate. Votes were contributed by students in the class as well as student listeners in other classes who used the podcasts as resources in their own work with *Ender's Game*.

The bar for what a podcast could do was set by a group of five students whom Kristen described as "smart kids who truly came out of nowhere to own this project." To prepare the content for their podcast, they used AOL chat and Twitter to solicit questions that their peers (and others in their Twitter networks) had while reading *Ender's Game*. After generating a list of the questions that were the most pressing or which were echoed by several peers, the group devised three segments to their show. The first was modeled on the NPR radio show Car Talk. Instead of fielding questions about car maintenance, students created a skit in which readers called upon "Click and Clunk" (names which played on both the content of the NPR show *and* a self-monitoring reading strategy beloved by the building's reading specialist) for suggestions and response to their reading questions. The second segment featured interviews of two student readers, highlighting different interpretations of the same scene. The third segment was an advertisement for the sequel to *Ender's Game* (which group members discovered and all read when completing research to support their show). Other podcasts included creative content ranging from Skype interviews of readers working with *Ender's Game* (one of which featured a graduate of Kristen's class who spoke about how the text connected to the reading he was now doing in his tenth-grade classes) to game show puzzles that were designed around key moments in the action of the novel.

Examining Practice

Kristen was surprised by students' engagement as readers throughout the literature circles and the podcast creation. She explained, "It wasn't about the technology. They spoke of amplifying their work as readers because they were doing something with [their readings]—and there was a certain level of 'public-ness' in what is usually a private, individual task." Many students spoke of their growth as readers, as Paula shared, "I am more a reader than I thought I was, especially when I now hear it." Kristen noted that their approaches as readers were markedly different in this work; "they were reading in more attentive ways, looking for moments where their own comprehension was shaky, or looking for opportunities to talk with peers about what was happening as they worked with the text." While she saw movements in students' work in the traditional casting of the literature circle projects, she noted that students in this class were practicing significantly more self-regulation than she'd expected or seen in the other classes.

In contemplating why this might have been the case, Kristen moved away from thinking about the technology and toward thinking about the opportunities and implicit scaffolds present in the collaborative assignment. She explained, "When you read on your own, or even when you read and share ideas in a book circle, it is still for individual goals. Here, there was a collective energy—kids read for themselves, their understanding, and to contribute to an end product that they wanted to be present in." The AL Brief speaks often about the importance of students' confidence as readers and writers, holding that it is a critical asset for those instances in which content becomes more challenging. It also defines engagement in terms that implicitly require confidence, holding that "engaged adolescents demonstrate internal motivation, self-efficacy, and a desire for mastery" (4).

The community of readers and writers that emerged through this task was an outcome Kristen had hoped to see. She explained, "You know this from all of our earlier talks, this is a biggie. And I saw kids come together here who don't usually . . . and who were actually working together." She attributed that to the "hook" of the authenticity of the work, but she also spoke of the importance of feedback:

> You see what they do online in ranking and rating what they see and hear. To replicate that here added another layer of communication, and I really believe that it impacted how kids wanted to come together to create something that would receive that kind of response. No one wants to create something that doesn't get heard or that doesn't do what was intended. The stakes were raised, and my favorite part of that is that they did it themselves.

[handwritten margin note: Positive outcomes of the podcasting]

Bruner writes about community as a place within which a student learns but where his or her understanding is constructed as part of a group who share his interests. There were multiple layers to this community in Kristen's classroom, ranging from the communities within the literature circle to the community of readers across the team who were reading *Ender's Game* and using the podcasts as learning resources.

As Kristen looked across the podcasts and the work students demonstrated in the classroom, one characteristic emerged that was strikingly different from the classes that did the visual/gallery walk project. She explained, "Re-reading. It was happening all the time here. Kids walked around with their books. It wasn't required, but it was necessary. In the other work, it was good to do, but not as critical." Students attributed this to their roles in their work. As Hank explained, "If I'm going to have something to say about it that other people are listening to, and that they can listen to again, I've got to have it right. A presentation is one shot. A podcast is as many shots as you choose to listen [to]." In this work, Kristen and Hank spoke of the technology as merely a tool for composing that opened up other roles and responsibilities for readers and writers.

The podcasts also drove home the message that all readers assign different meanings to texts. This was first experienced as the literature circle groups came together to discuss the novel but was amplified as students listened across the podcasts to the emerging and differing readings of the novel. Kristen explained this through the lens of a teacher who wanted to move the thinking of all levels of readers in her classroom. "Skilled readers need to wrestle against alternative readings, and my developing or reluctant readers need their readings to be affirmed as long as they can be explained and supported." The podcast activity functioned as an implicit scaffold for this level of interpretive work and meaning-making.

Kristen describes teaching as often a practice of making hard choices. Despite Kristen's beliefs in constructivist practice and creating spaces for students to follow their own lines of inquiry, this was an opportunity that, at times, pushed outside of her comfort zone. She explained, "It wasn't about time—as they stayed in that box. I think it was more that I was seeing what could happen when I backed out and let them show how they were smart and what they were learning—and do so on their own terms, not just through their own media." The brief espouses the need for teaching adolescents in a way that creates "caring, responsive classroom environments that enable students to take ownership of literacy activities" (4). For Kristen, this happened, but she continually emphasized that it was difficult work. And it was this challenge that led her to affirm and celebrate her instincts to slow down and work with just one class at a time. She explained, "We don't do technology-related work every day, every week, or even within every unit. I try in little bits as it lets me look closely at what is happening. If I start big, it usually doesn't end well. I go from instinct."

On the Horizon

Today's youth, by participating in the design of multimodal texts, could well be invigorating a literate tradition that has stood the test of time and shows no sign of abatement because the available means of signification are multiplying.

—Hull & Nelson

This chapter argues for what is possible when we open up what counts as valued communication in the classroom, engage students in practices that affirm their multiple literacies, and move them successfully through tasks that require that they also exercise keen print literacies. Teaching with new literacies doesn't remove us from the realities of assessments that value discrete bits of knowledge or that confine our students to writing five-paragraph essays that include no more than forty sentences, but it does provide us with an opportunity to push up against those assessments by providing students with opportunities to demonstrate what they know in different modes, media, outcomes, and communities of learners.

The exciting thing about work that provides students with the opportunity to express what they are coming to know and understand through a variety of modes or tools or media is that we provide them with the opportunity to produce something unexpected, new, and genuinely creative. We foster their confidence. We encourage innovation. We model for students that learning and knowledge isn't a tangible "thing" but an activity. To me, that is one of the energies within our discipline that smart teachers know how to tap. And, again, we do so in a way that affords students new entrances into literary interpretation and language study.

New literacies and Web 2.0 tools make it possible for *anyone* to engage in the art of filmmaking, photography, composing, etc. They make it possible for Kristen's students to share a digital narrative of their reading of a text or a podcast of ideas emerging from their work with a novel. But perhaps more important, as the activities in this chapter exemplify, they present a new opportunity for exercising voice that is present in those media. On the horizon, if we are smart about our work and we learn from the ways that participatory media and social networks interrelate outside our classrooms, this kind of content creation will provide students with an opportunity to move from a private to a public voice, "helping students turn their self-expression into a form of public participation" (Rheingold 101). Kristen's class brushes close to this with the publishing of podcasts with the intent of using their knowledge to communicate with an engaged audience/listenership. We speak to be heard. With intention and purpose, as these students did, we speak to start a conversation. And, in that conversation, we can create change.

[handwritten margin note: ✻ private → public voice]

In This Chapter . . .

Book Projects with VoiceThread

Technologies used:

VoiceThread (www.voicethread.com)

A note: I recommend that you look at the educator's accounts within Voice-Thread that allow for more options and moderation. These can be found at ed.voicethread.com. I'm impressed any time that folks at a website take it upon themselves to think deeply about the ways that young readers and writers can learn and grow through using their tool. It also leads me to have more trust that this is a tool that will likely stick around.

Where to go for more information:
- A teacher compiled list of classroom exemplar VoiceThreads, http://voicethread4education.wikispaces.com
- "How to" resources, http://ed.voicethread.com/help/manuals
- VoiceThread digital library, http://ed.voicethread.com/library
- An article in *Edutopia*, http://www.edutopia.org/voicethread-interactive-multimedia-albums

Podcasting with Gcast

Technologies used:
- Gcast–www.gcast.com
- Audacity–http://audacity.sourceforge.net

Where to go for more information:
- Common craft video about podcasting, http://www.commoncraft.com/podcasting
- Kathy Schrock's list of valuable links supporting podcasting in the classroom, http://school.discoveryeducation.com/schrockguide/gadgets.html
- An idea list I return to regularly for inspiration, http://www.speedofcreativity.org/2006/09/01/kidscast-exciting-podcasting-activities-to-promote-research-and-learning
- The "podcasting" toolbox, http://mashable.com/2007/07/04/podcasting-toolbox

A tip: While there are many, many classrooms across the globe "broadcasting" content through podcasts, it can often be difficult to find models to help inform your planning. I tend to rely on iTunes to find them. Use the search tools from the podcasting page and look under "education."

Writing Together: Participatory Media, Collaboration, and the English Classroom

> Nobody is as smart as everybody.
> —Kevin Kelly

Situating the Conversation

Eleventh-grade students at Banks High School cycled through the library/media center at the start of their unit on media literacy. Set up as a series of learning stations, the unit rotated students through viewing film clips from recent PBS programs examining youth media practices, cruising the stacks for available material on Internet safety, meeting with staff who shared strategies for evaluating online information, and, at the small lab at the rear corner of the library, meeting for a discussion on the kinds of media they were using and a critical examination of why and how they were drawn to those spaces.

Students started this discussion with an online poll that provided them some anonymity while spurring and encouraging a rich discussion. Using polleverywhere.com, students responded to the poll's questions through either the laptops available in this lab or text messaging on their cell phones. Because we were interested in the ways students were working as readers and writers in online spaces, the questions started there, asking, "Are you a writer?" Students had two choices for response—yes or no. Of the 217 students who cycled through that station over the course of two days, 203 replied "yes."

In the questions that followed, they shared their collective ideas about the differences between writing in school and writing outside of school; writing expository essays and writing in a blog; and writing for a teacher and writing for an expanded, more authentic audience. The questions and results in the poll were conversation starters, yielding opportunities for follow-up and, more important, students' explanations, challenges, and celebrations. Given that an overwhelming majority of the students had described themselves as writers, it was surprising that less than half (94 of 217) identified themselves as engaged writers when in school but that more than three-quarters saw themselves (183 of 217) as engaged when writing outside of school.

As students set out to discuss their practices with new media in terms of how we shape them/how they shape us, the list of the spaces in which students were working outside of the classroom was lengthy, including but not limited to weblogs, wikis, Facebook, instant messaging, chat rooms, and fanfiction sites. But more interesting was the list of reasons behind their engagement as writers in these spaces. Students spoke about the importance of following their own interests, avoiding what Seema called "the box that every prompt I write about in school puts me in." They wrote online to connect with one another and, as Peter shared, "to put my ideas out there and get a response from other writers or just kids who care about the same stuff." And they believed that their teachers didn't care about what made any of their media spaces work. As Lexie offered, "Typing a journal entry in a blog doesn't make it a blog post. It's like my teachers think that if we change from a word document to a wiki or blog, that they're doing something different. They don't get it."

I didn't take their ideas to mean that it was time to abandon the traditional writing assignments that are core to our discipline. But as I listened, I realized that just moving traditional curricular tasks into new media spaces isn't helpful or purposive work. Instead, we need to make these changes with an eye to how authentic writing in new media spaces actually differs from our traditional work. And we need to leverage the characteristics of and new capacities within the digital writing spaces we bring into our teaching. Shirky argues, "We are living in the middle of the largest increase in expressive capability in the human race" (106). Beginning there presents new challenges and opportunities not only for our curriculum but also, more important, for our work with student writers.

As noted in the AL Brief, the research on student writing provides evidence both of what isn't happening and some possible openings for engaging and motivating student writers in new ways. The brief shares data indicating "40 percent of high school seniors never write or rarely write a paper of three or more pages, and although fourth and eighth graders showed some improvement in writing between 1998 and 2002, the scores of twelfth graders showed no significant change" (1). Several studies examine the role that computers and technology play in student writing, finding that students who regularly write with computers are more likely to collaborate with peers through both providing and receiving feedback (Goldberg et al. 20). They also identify a resulting increase in student motivation and the length and quality of work (Goldberg et al. 15).

The Pew Internet and American Life Projects' recent work on adolescent writers echoes some of what I learned at Banks High School, that 93 percent of teens write for pleasure and 85 percent believe that good writing is important to their success outside the classroom (Lenhart et al., "Writing"). However, though they found that 85 percent of adolescents aged 12–17 engage in some form of digital communication, only 60 percent of those same adolescents think of this work as "writing" (Lenhart et al., "Writing"). In speaking about what prompts them to write, students' lists included "writing to make something happen, writing to achieve a desired goal, writing to get a grade, and writing to express emotions" (Lenhart et al., "Writing").

Research tells us that adolescents are largely learning how to mediate identity, compose, and collaborate in online spaces outside of our classrooms, and that these are practices and spaces that are increasingly valued, and even expected, by employers. Teaching that incorporates, models, and challenges work in communicating within new media spaces provides students with a different degree of knowing. The English class that encourages all students to engage, write, and collaborate with digital media does not replace traditional academic writing. Instead, it challenges us to help students become readers and writers who can "interpret, use, and produce live, electronic, and paper texts that employ linguistic, visual, auditory, gestural, and spatial semiotic systems for social, political, cultural, civic, and economic purpose in socially and culturally diverse contexts" (Anstey and Bull 41).

Using new media spaces to communicate and collaborate works differently from the print practices embedded deeply into our curriculum. When writers are online, publishing and audience can be immediate. Shirky explains that "The act of publishing [was once] limited to a tiny fraction of the population. . . . [N]ow, once a user connects to the Internet, he has access to a platform that is at once global and free" (77). When online, we are positioned to share more ideas with more people through a variety of media. This is a reality that puts new pressures on the print-only practices reflected in much of our English curricula. And when the pressures are placed at the right space at the right time, we create real openings in what we do to foster purposeful, smart communication within an authentic community.

Connections to the NCTE Adolescent Literacy Brief

Writing and Collaborating within New Media

- **Requires continual learning and identity development.**

  "Literacy learning is an ongoing and non-hierarchical process." (2)

  "Adolescents rely on literacy in their identity development, using reading and writing to define themselves as persons." (2)

- **Helps create points of connection between what it means to create and collaborate outside of school and inside the more traditional English curriculum.**

  "Adolescents already have access to many different discourses, including those of ethnic, online, and popular culture communities." (3)

  "Adolescents are successful when they understand that texts are written in social settings and for social purposes." (3)

- **Provides opportunities for relevant, purposeful work.**

  "Experiences with task-mastery enable increased self-efficacy, which leads to continued engagement." (4)

  "Using technology is one way to provide learning-centered, relevant activities." (4)

The AL Brief encourages us to think deeply about the opportunities within our curriculum for students to authentically collaborate and, when possible, put their knowledge into action (see sidebar). This chapter examines one teacher's work alongside her students to foster their skills in working across media and digital genres in order to better work within an online community. As in the earlier chapters, we'll use the brief to take apart what happens in the classroom, to learn from the perspective of a grounded yet innovative teacher, and to explore what students were able to accomplish as engaged readers and writers working in an environment that brought together face-to-face engagement and participation in a digital environment.

From a Teacher's Point of View: Real Reasons to Write

Megan is an eleventh-grade English teacher at Banks High School. She teaches three classes per day on an alternating block schedule. While this provides students with ninety minutes of English class, the schedule has been an adjustment for Megan and her students who, up until this semester, followed a seven-period day. She has taught at Banks High School for fourteen years, working each year with on-level and honors-level students. Her department values collaboration and professional learning, regularly engaging in lesson study and weekly lunches exploring strategies from professional reading.

Banks High is part of a districtwide laptop initiative, equipping every classroom teacher with a laptop (refreshed every two years) and an LCD projector. Two labs are available by reservation to eleventh-grade English teachers in addition to the two labs in the library. Though a resource-rich environment, multiple "gatekeepers" in the building enact a policy of limiting access to websites (unless teachers demonstrate its educational value), limiting each class to a total number of days in the computer lab (no matter if the lab subsequently remains empty), and controlling access to the digital cameras, digital video cameras, Elmo projectors, and other tools available for teachers to check out for classroom use. As a result, technology use is not widespread given the work involved in gaining access to needed tools or teaching spaces.

Matching Pedagogies with New Tools: Reinventing the Character Journal

One component of Megan's former work with *The Great Gatsby* required that students develop a "point of view" character journal. In the journal students were asked to take on the voice of a character from the novel (typically assigned randomly as students entered class on a day before they began reading), using daily entries to retell some aspect of the action in the pages included in that day's assignment. Across the full novel, journals would, when done well, provide a creative insight into students' reading while requiring that they write descriptively and develop consistent, well-supported interpretations.

Using the framework used throughout this book, Megan rethought this assignment, arranging her thinking in three areas:

1. I am doing _____ well but can do better.

2. What watching my students' literacy practices teaches me that I want to build upon: _____ .

3. _____ isn't working.

Even though the character journal was an assignment listed in the district curricular guide and, as such, didn't feel like an idea she owned, Megan enjoyed how the journals encouraged students to construct meaning throughout their reading. She explained, "Students need to continually 'retool' the voice of their characters as they learn more throughout their reading and, in some cases, when their predictions run wrong." And, though she celebrates the ways in which the journals evoke rich interpretive skills, she did offer a confession. "I know that this is something teachers don't say. This is a project that I really don't enjoy reading. No matter how brilliant the kid, and they are regularly creative here, it feels too much like a school project and not enough like good writing grown from deep reading."

[handwritten margin note: "School" project]

Megan knew exactly what she wanted to move from students' new literacies practices into the assignment. She shared, "I'm always struck by the ways that my students document things through pictures. Sure, I've always kept albums, but these guys have cameras or phones up and at the ready for every event." Bigger than the work of taking pictures are the ways in which students shared their images. She explained, "It isn't like we just put photos online to get them off of our computers or memory sticks. We do it for the same reason we show people albums when they come to our homes. It is sharing our point of view, sharing our experience, and sharing a story." In thinking about that practice in the

context of the journal assignment, Megan was adamant that this was part of the
problem in her reluctance as a reader: "a collection of images works collectively. . . .
So, I view one and then see the second through the lens created by the first. In the
journal writing, kids wrote and then moved on to the second. The connection isn't
there." Apart from the content of the journal, she also saw potential in the idea of
audience. She explained, "Kids write these for me and only for me. That seems to
be rare in the writing they do outside of the classroom. Even photo sites like Flickr
or Photobucket have options for sharing, commenting, coming together."

What challenged Megan the most about this assignment were the ways her
most reluctant students consistently disengaged from the project. She'd tried to use
graphic organizers to help develop their thinking. She'd tried providing incre-
mental feedback or using peer review to help encourage the writing. Finally, she
came to the conclusion that the problem was rooted in the same place as her own
reluctance to read students' work. She shared, "There it was, like a big light in my
face. . . . This was a completely school-only kind of project. And, with my more
reluctant kids, I need to be able to say 'here's how this really matters.' I could do
that about the reading but not about this project. In fact, it is even more telling
that they never even asked."

Engaging Student Writers

In an attempt to move the assignment closer to the kind of visual documentary
work that she believed would engage more students, Megan revised the assignment
to be one steeped in visual content. To start, she looked to a tool/environment in
which she had comfort as a user—flickr.com. She'd worked with friends throughout the past year to participate in "Project 365," a prompt in Flickr challenging
users to take and post one (and only one) photo per day that represents that day.
To be a part of the project, photos were tagged with "project365," allowing participants in the group to look across and within the image collection. She explained,
"This was one of those times that drove home what it meant to explore a common
idea or event from different perspectives." When posting an image to Flickr, users
have two options which allowed for writing: one, using the caption space; or, two,
embedding comments in rollover boxes placed on the image by "adding a note"
using the toolbar appearing above the image.

Bringing together bits of Project 365 and her own instructional goals, Megan
created a "15-Day Visual Character Journal." Students would capture one image
for each day of reading, again from the point of view of a character from the novel,
but now summarizing or capturing a key moment from the events in the pages
of the assigned reading. Posts to the class "group" in Flickr were to consist of an
image, a caption written from the character's point of view, and two specific tags

unique to the class. Tags were meant to help organize entries, as well as to provide students with a quick way to access and look across one another's images. Entries were titled according to a specific formula (again meant to help with organization): Character's Name, Number of Posting/Number of Total Posts Required. So, for example, a post might be titled "Jay Gatsby 2/15" (signaling that this is the second of fifteen posts).

This was mostly an "out-of-class" activity, just as the original character journal was. While she typically was concerned about assigning homework requiring the use of a computer, Megan was less anxious about this work, explaining, "I polled the class and all but one of my students have access to a digital camera or cell phone. And I can easily supply one to my student through our media center." When it came to accessing Flickr, after making a request to the building technology specialist, the site was opened for student access on the computers in the media center. Megan explained, "Even if students didn't have a computer to write from at home, they could use ones here that would certainly get the job done." And because storing images in Flickr meant that images could be accessed from any computer with an Internet connection, students had much more range in where they'd be able to work.

Apart from the technology, Megan wanted this project to push students to move deeply into their reading while also using the reading to see their community in a different way. As she explained, "That is one thing from grad school that I still remember when it comes to my own reading [of] . . . Freire. . . . I want them to read the word to read the world around us. And, if that works right, it should push back. They should read the world to read the word."

Sharing and Evaluating Images and Posts

Not only was Megan eager to see what students created, but also students were equally interested in one another's work. "From the first submissions or posts, kids were asking one another to see their images, not just because they were being social, but because they were interested in better understanding character." The community grew quickly across classes and was evident in the emerging comments left by peers at the bottom of their image posts in Flickr. Although it was an unintended part of the work, Megan felt it best to keep the commenting a natural and kid-driven part of the project. "Writers need lots of readers and if I get in there, I'm afraid that might stop. So I'm watching and reading but not assessing or mandating that they now all write comments, too."

Megan found that class discussions emerged from the images and that, counter to the print journal writing, the journals became a text read and explored in class alongside the novel. She explained, "Students referenced one another's work,

[handwritten margin note: Teacher role w/ comments]

talked about divergent opinions and readings, and even talked about how you'd need to revise an image as you learned something later in the book that made the first reading no longer work." Megan was further pleased that participation in the work and resulting discussion was not limited to the skilled readers in the class. Instead, she shared that there were some students for whom their images and posts created an entrance into the discussion:

> Hannah in third period has a photographer's eye, so perspective in her work is compelling by itself—but when kids consider she is working from the point of view of Myrtle Wilson, it opens up a whole other layer. So, they draw Hannah into the discussion—an entrance that she has blossomed with but that she needed them to create.

The work of creating images consistently pushed students back into rereading the text multiple times, encouraging them to revisit earlier passages to inform the creation of the next image. As Scott, a student in the fifth-period group shared, "I'm thinking my way through this project, and I'm not one to do that. But I want to make sure that the picture isn't just a pic. I want it to show what I think." Further, students engaged in the kind of connective writing that Megan had identified as missing in the print character journals. She explained, "The images and posts built from one another and captured that 'story' that made the old way feel disconnected and disjointed."

Examining Practice

As happens with any activity that we put into the hands of actual kids, Megan saw areas for continued development when she next implemented the unit. The first had to do with the tagging structure. She explained, "Kids were more interested in looking across their peers' work with similar characters than I'd expected. So, next time, the character's name as a tag would help in that." Further, she planned to fold in a reflective writing component. "Students were doing such interesting work. I wanted to slow them down, get them thinking about how they were composing with images and their writing, and to tie to specific lines that evoked the images." She emphasized, "These aren't areas where things didn't work. They are places where things worked so much better than I'd anticipated that I want to take it to the next step."

The AL Brief compels teachers to consider the ways in which new media practices can work to support students' work in accessing disciplinary content. So, through that lens, the work of generating and revising one's reading through a process of writing through images and then receiving feedback from an invested community with shared goals provides students with opportunities to leverage their literacies in order to unlock the complex discourse of literary analysis and interpretation. Megan's goal of engaging students who struggled as readers and writers was

[handwritten margin note: areas for improvement in flickr project]

supported by her acknowledgment of different ways of showing what they knew but also in providing an implicit "prompt in which students reflect on their current understandings, questions, and learning processes to help improve their learning" (3).

As much as this was work that motivated her more reluctant readers, it did so through the appeal of the mode of expression and the desire to participate in a community, as seen in Hannah's comments and in comments shared through-out the classes. Megan celebrated the steps this reflected while wrestling with whether this was the kind of relevant task she'd hoped for. She explained, "I know that my students engage differently when they see the work as more than just a school project or as a task that will help them develop skills that matter outside of the classroom." As much as Megan, and I, and most English teachers looking at the assignment celebrate the kind of close, intentional reading that the task requires, relevance to Megan was more about using the work students did in Flickr to do something that had meaning outside of the English classroom as well. She explained, "I know we're closer, and for this project, I think that we've gone far enough, unless we were to share our images with a broader audience. But for what I want with relevance, we need to be authentic to participatory media in a more authentic way." Further, she felt that Flickr had been a good tool for connecting students, but she was now ready to think about what it might mean to foster and engage in collaborative work.

Matching Pedagogies with New Tools: Writing Collaboratively

Later in the year, Megan developed a completely new project as a cumulative task during students' work with *Othello*. This was her first time teaching the play, so the three layers of questions I encouraged her to use to unpack her thinking didn't fit the case. In previous years, this unit had focused around the comedy *Much Ado about Nothing*. Given the ways that working with a different text created new possibilities, she found her thinking to be more open. "This is a first draft," she explained. "I'm not locked by something that didn't work. I know the text. I know my students. And I think I know a way to bring the two together and hit some of my earlier goals with collaboration paired with rigor." Since the character journal activity, students had not engaged in any assignment in her class asking for the use of technology. She explained, "It isn't every day, and I had to figure out the puzzle from the last [task] in order to see what would come next."

Combining Expertise

Megan's assignment began as an opportunity for students to work throughout their reading of the play to assemble resources or artifacts that demonstrate their progress and what they were coming to know. To that end, she developed a class wiki and invited students to post their assigned work and to participate in the discussion and FAQ pages in order to support one another through a challenging text. Assigned work included a video of a "modernized" scene; a scan of a visual "open mind" of Othello, Iago, or Desdemona at three different points of action in the play (Burke 146); and two samples of reflective writing from their reader's/writer's notebooks. In thinking about the purpose behind these assignments, Megan shared, "I wanted students to have a repository from which they could interact with one another but also explore how their peers were constructing meaning as we read." This was level one.

Level two of the project began after students had finished reading the play and once Megan had seen evidence that the wiki was being used as more than a storage container. Students had been regularly posting their work, and several had started a few robust pages of discussion, one of which embedded clips (from YouTube) of different film versions of Desdemona's final moments along with students' analysis and reviews of which most accurately captured the scene as they'd envisioned it. She explained, "I didn't need to see scads of participation. I just wanted to see some interest and if students referenced it as a resource as we studied the play—which they certainly did."

The next stage of the project required students to revisit their wiki, this time combining their collective expertise into a resource that would be useful to other students reading the play. Megan had posted a call in Global SchoolNet for an English class studying the play in time to use the resource and found a collaborator in a class in Missouri. She explained, "I think that this was part of what I learned from our earlier work. I wanted students to assemble what they knew—which is connective—but I really wanted them to use it to collaboratively create a usable and used resource. I just didn't know that yet." Students met this new challenge with mixed response. For some, it was intimidating to think that their work was going to help other students work through a text that had stretched so much of their own skills to "get through." For others, it meant taking down a piece of their work from the class wiki (of which they were really proud) in order to support something different. As these were reactions that the class addressed together, Megan and her students had opportunities to co-construct a plan that would both provide multiple points of engagement for students who were hesitant to make another pass at the book and affirm the work already done by developing a new public site and keeping the class site stable. Megan explained, "All of our work up until now has allowed us to be that kind of a community and for students to buy it when I say that we're in it together."

(handwritten margin notes: "Wiki example" and "rationale for wiki")

Constructing and Sharing a Multimodal Reader's Guide

The work of building the class wiki was as simple as registering a site within PbWiki (a free wiki tool that affords layers of monitoring and protections that make collaborative writing a realistic option for a secondary class). So, across Megan's six classes, this meant URLs for six separate wikis—each beginning with text to signify the school, *Othello* at the center, and the class number at the end. For example, a site URL from first period would read bhsothello1.pbwiki.com. Keeping those consistent was helpful to her management and students' eventual work in looking across sites once they completed their construction.

Bringing together students' expertise meant providing a space for some students to speak as skillful readers of the text, others to work as savvy researchers, and still others to bring their multimodal compositing skills to bear. After Megan brainstormed possible contents with each class, students divided into collaborative groups to create/generate specific content while three students (deemed the "project managers" given their roles in compiling materials and designing the framework, organization, and menus of the wiki) helped Megan in circulating around the groups to assist in growing ideas, supporting work, and troubleshooting. Megan described the work as different from most group projects. "The whole class had a goal and, because they knew that their evaluation was being done by peers in another state who needed their resources to help move them through a difficult text, I saw them come together in unique ways."

Students had three ninety-minute classes for collaborative meetings, collective composing, and face-to-face work on completing the wiki. To Megan, this was a massive amount of instructional time, but time that she usually spent viewing different versions of the film or in working on a formal essay. She explained:

> Since most of the videos were embedded onto the wiki, that became an embedded part of our early discussions, especially as students had pulled them as necessary resources to talk about while reading. . . . With the exception of one class period, we're doing this within the same amount of time that I'd allocated to the Shakespeare unit in previous years.

Assessment of the wikis involved three layers: one, peer feedback from the collaborating classes (here, rating the usefulness, appeal, and accuracy of site content but mostly providing feedback through posted comments to resources and a dedicated page on each wiki); two, teacher feedback from both Megan and the collaborative teacher; and, three, self-evaluation requiring students to evaluate their contributions, their understanding of the text, and their work in the group. Megan offered, "There is feedback coming from all directions with this. It's a lot to take in, but that is a different problem, and I think a welcome one, from just hearing from me."

3 layers of wiki assessment

An example of how this wiki project worked well grew out of the collaborations within third period. As this was the class with the broadest range of student interests and reading levels, Megan was initially concerned that the class might need more scaffolding and supports to finally develop their wiki. Though the group took more time to "gel" around the items brainstormed in their initial list, they were also the single group to grow that list in other directions once the work and creative energies got moving. Their wiki included what across the classes were standard items, such as character lists, plot summaries, etc. The creative content included wordia.com-style videos for key vocabulary, a screencast of their critical reading of a SparkNotes page that was "missing key information," a set of tags within del.icio.us where they'd located and grouped resources on the play, and even a pool of Flickr images of their own enacted tableaux from key scenes (which grew to include those of the three classes who used their wiki as a resource). Megan shared, "There is nothing like those rare instances when you see kids surprise themselves. What a takeaway."

Examining Practice

Megan set out to challenge students to work more closely with the text, drilling deeply into areas that their class discussion might have touched upon, but to do so while combining expertise to create an outcome that mattered outside of their classroom walls. She credited the success of the work to the ways in which students received and generated feedback. "They commented on one another's work rapidly and far more critically than I could have, but, bigger than that, they worked with the knowledge that if they hit it right, they'd be receiving the kind of feedback they wanted from peers—'your work helped me.'" This wasn't work about a grade. Instead, as the AL Brief suggests, it was the result of learner-centered opportunities that "connect writing practices with real-world experiences and tasks" (4).

Apart from the technology and multimodal composing that engaged students in this project, students spoke of being engaged in a different kind of writing—writing that was "purposeful." Megan explained, "They talked about their writing in the wiki as writing that wasn't about school but that was about learning and, as second period said, 'holding up other readers.'" Moreover, they used their writing to fuel additional readings of the play, developing into a recursive cycle of discovery, reading, and writing. As such, students were exercising practices as engaged readers and writers, and, for many, building critical levels of confidence needed for subsequent learning in and outside of the classroom.

On the Horizon

Talking helps you know, but using helps you understand.
> —Ewan McIntosh

Megan's teaching created media opportunities through which her students could engage in meaning-making, in composing, in creating, in sharing, in commenting, in collaborating, and in pushing their knowledge forward. As Rheingold writes, "Creativity has always been a highly collaborative, cumulative, and social activity in which people with different skills, points of view, and insights, share and develop ideas together" (n. pag.). Through their creative work in Flickr, their wiki, and the myriad tools/media spaces where they created content shared through the wiki, students were able to show how they were smart while further developing their literate identities in ways that are significant both to the English curriculum as we've known it and the new literacies-informed English curriculum we're working to design.

As I've argued in other chapters, we can't assume that all of our students come to us richly literate in varied new media practices, in much the same way as we don't assume that they come to us with a history of "sustained experiences with diverse texts in a variety of genres that offer multiple perspectives of life experiences" (AL Brief 4). Megan's work isn't dripping in bleeding-edge technologies, but it does grow from media she understands from her own use. It is situated in an almost ubiquitous tool, yet innovatively framed by hooks that tie to what we know about the literacies needed to engage students mindfully and meaningfully in new media learning spaces. In doing so, she establishes a frame allowing students degrees of autonomy, follows their self-directed lines of inquiry, and assists in connecting them to an invested network. So, no matter what students bring into Megan's class, they have engaged in practices that better equip them not to jump into Facebook chatter but to use participatory media to leverage expertise in creating meaningful work.

In This Chapter . . .

Using Flickr with Character Journals

Technologies used:

Flickr (www.flickr.com)

A note: Use this as an opportunity to teach students about copyright and intellectual property by also teaching them how to work with creative commons licensing when posting their own work.

Where to go for more information:

- A video on online photo sharing, http://www.commoncraft.com/photosharing
- The "help forum" within the Flickr site, http://www.flickr.com/help
- A partnership effort between Flickr and the Library of Congress, http://www.flickr.com/commons
- One of the smartest uses of Flickr to support student learning was designed by Darren Kuropatwa, a math teacher in Canada. The task asks students to find images of math concepts in play in the world and landscape outside of the classroom. The rubric (also included at this link) is a solid model of how we think about assessing kids' digital work. http://adifference.blogspot.com/2006/12/flickr-assignment-rubric-v10-were-out.html

Using a Class Wiki

Technologies used:

PbWiki–www.pbworks.com

Where to go for more information:

- A "how to" video, http://www.commoncraft.com/video-wikis-plain-english.
- Classroom 2.0 resource guide on using wikis, http://wiki.classroom20.com/Wikis
- A community of wiki-using teachers, http://wikisineducation.wetpaint.com
- As there are many, many wiki tools available, this site is helpful in making a choice across the options, http://www.wikimatrix.org/wizard.php
- I first learned about wikis from watching Vicki Davis's smart uses in her classroom, http://coolcatteacher.blogspot.com/2005/12/wiki-wiki-teaching-art-of-using-wiki.html
- A chapter worth reading: Richardson, W. Wikis: Easy collaboration for all. *Blogs, podcasts, wikis, and other powerful web tools for classrooms.* 2nd ed. Sage: Corwin Press, 2008

Conclusion: On the Horizon

> When a technology becomes normal, then ubiquitous, and finally so pervasive as to be invisible, that is when the really profound changes happen, and for today's youth, our new social tools have passed normal and are heading to ubiquitous. And, the invisible is coming.
>
> —Clay Shirky (105)

Thinking about Change

Like most readers, I have a stack of books, journals, and other texts that make up a "need to read soon" pile. The stack grows throughout the year, not because I'm not reading, but because I'm adding to the list faster than I move through it. There are some writers, however, whose work leaps to the top of the stack and some whose work never even makes it into the pile as I push everything else aside to delve into it. It's a bit of a leap-frog process that happens when a new text intersects with a project or, more likely, a hunger for a particular voice or genre at a given time. That brings me to this morning when I came across an article by Margaret Weigel, Carrie

Reminds me so much of my own TBR pile

James, and Howard Gardner addressing learning in the twenty-first century. I stepped away from email, turned off the ringer on my cell phone, and eagerly, happily, read.

Why Gardner? His work sits at the roots of my learning to teach. I once turned to his work on multiple intelligences to help me engage differently with the talents and learning interests of the students in my classroom. His ideas have challenged me to think differently about creativity, engagement, ingenuity, and, now, with this work, the ways in which new literacies and new media make possible and even necessary some rethinking of what we do and how.

The article offers a history of school and schooling, focusing on learning experiences and examining "how competences are purveyed via the media of the time" (Weigel et al. n. pag.). As a reader, I found it affirming to see some of the observations I'd made as a teacher present in the article; that the content and function of school as we know it has stayed relatively stable despite the changes that have occurred outside of our school walls; and that goal of education, now and then, sits in fostering skills that help students become engaged, participating citizens of a now global community mediating and negotiating information through the lens of specific disciplines while being responsible to a profession and one's community. And to disregard the ways in which new media are creating new learning opportunities and literacy practices is to keep curricula in the box that says all kids will grow from the same set texts, experiences, and media.

As I read, I turned once more to *Adolescent Literacy: An NCTE Policy Research Brief*, in part because I was deeply into revisions of this book, but mostly because of the areas of connection emerging across the two documents. If we read the brief just as a summary of research, we miss the big picture: that it captures and articulates ways that our field and profession need to grow in order to successfully do the work we value, helping students to work as intentional, self-directed learners who skillfully construct meaning from and with a range of texts and share that knowledge and understanding in meaningful ways. It challenges us to see our students in new ways, valuing the literacies they bring into our classrooms both to engage and build points of connection bridging students into the academic work of our discipline. And, if we read closely, it offers suggestions about ways that our work can continue to grow in meaning and impact.

I continued to read the two articles, placing them side by side on my desk. As Weigel et al. discuss the importance of preparing students to learn literacy practices for a lifetime "to successfully learn, synthesize, and adjust to rapidly shifting requirements of the workplace and the culture" (n. pag.), the brief emphasizes that "literacy learning is an ongoing and non-hierarchical process" (2). And, where the brief values instruction in which students and teachers co-construct literacy practices and engage in inquiry-driven work, the article speaks of the importance of instructional models that "elicit more engagement and investment on the part of the learner, and less overt control and knowledge dissemination on the part of the educator" (n. pag.). Both emphasize the importance of engaging in social learning, extending collaborations, providing feedback, and engaging in opportunities to use literacies "for social and political purposes as [we] create meanings and participate in shaping [our] immediate environments" (NCTE 3).

Where the article takes a different path is in forecasting the changes in learning, schooling, and literacy practices given what new media and new literacies practices are making possible today, reminding me that the brief was developed in 2007 and though it captures our imagination and holds significant truths, the literacy landscape outside of our classrooms has continued to develop and change. Gardner and his colleagues (Weigel et al.) argue that "digital media could be leveraged in ways that bring about a tipping point when learning becomes more decidedly individualized, constructivist, situated and social . . . and far too much of [our current] discussion centers on test scores in traditional subjects, secured in traditional ways" (n. pag.).

Thinking about Our Learning

As English teachers, we are in the thick of these shifting realities as our work begins in understanding how our students are literate and the literacy practices that they need to engage meaningfully and purposefully across disciplines and in disciplinary, local, and global communities outside of our classrooms. Further, the vision captured in the brief pushes the conversation about the roles of content, pedagogy, and assessment. The challenge is to take that vision into our teaching while also using our pedagogy and students' growth to keep the conversation moving in ways that capture the realities and the futures of our work. The chapters in this book have meant to share stories of teachers who are doing just that, but to do so in a way that illuminates how the AL Brief can function as a tool for exploring and informing your own practice.

I think of the brief as a story starter, prompting us to carry ideas forward in anchored and intentional ways. As I explained earlier, this is a process of examining our teaching; seeing our students; thinking critically about new tools, practices, and media; and finding small ways to maximize the intersections. It isn't about urgent technology use. It is about emergent use of a new literacies practice or new media to move students in ways that aren't possible with "traditional" practices. We don't roll in the technology because it will "motivate" kids by its simple presence in the room. We examine their practices. We learn about what makes new media and the literacy practices they evoke and make possible unique, different, and compelling. We think critically about the negative potentials of digital media for learning. And,

[handwritten marginalia: Gardner comment on digital media possibilities]

[handwritten marginalia: thoughts on technology and AL brief]

Continual
learning
examples

when we marry those capacities and literacies, we find rich and compelling areas of
our curriculum that are already ripe for our rethinking and retooling.

And to do this, we have to keep learning. There are resources that challenge and push my thinking, and I find them especially important as new literacies
learning *is* a social process. First, I engage in communities of practice that push my
thinking. This could be working alongside smart colleagues, attending conferences
(and engaging with the speakers who challenge my thinking), or copious reading.
Or, I think better, using digital media to inform and move my learning within a
community. As I mentioned earlier in this book, NCTE developed a Ning community to support teachers attending the 2008 conference, and has maintained
it given the ways in which teachers came together electronically for self-initiated
dialogue, sharing of materials and exemplars, and networking. Jim Burke then
developed a Ning community (englishcompanion.ning.com) after the conference
where teachers at all stages of their professional development are sharing models
of practice, questions emerging from their teaching, book recommendations, and
even engaging in electronic book groups around practitioner and trade books. I belong to these communities (and others) to keep fed, to learn with my colleagues but
to also "lurk" in discussions, soaking up the dialogue and participating when I'm
ready. And, work in a Ning environment can be as public or private as you'd like.
For example, in the professional development workshops I run, I encourage teachers who work to build community to continue that work online, setting up groups
in Ning protected by a password. Options abound. The key is to work alongside
professionals you respect to keep growing your thinking.

Beyond the texts discussed in the annotated bibliography of this book, there
are other print resources that I regularly turn to in order to move my thinking. I
read NCTE journals and other research and policy briefs to participate in the dialogue within our field. I subscribe to several blogs maintained by practicing teachers who are writing about their work. I use social bookmarking tools like de.licio.
us to share resources but to also look over the shoulder of trusted teachers and
thinkers to see what tools and resources they value. I read the *Learning and Leading
with Technology* and *Edutopia* journals for models of what other teachers are doing
across disciplines to engage students in new literacy practices with digital media.
And, each year I wait eagerly for the release of the *Horizon Report* which offers a
"forecast" of the media trends and emerging tools that are shaping learning spaces,
learning practices, and the next wave of tools under development. Looking at this
paragraph, it seems like a lot, but, just like the "to read" pile, there are times that I
move to one resource over another and times that I can't get to any of it. But it is
a way for me to push content to me, a skill I find increasingly important given the
mass of what is available and accessible.

suggested
journals

Learning Even When Things Don't Work

We all know that there are days where the technology bites back. As much as we plan with our pedagogy and student learning at the center and core of our work, there are days that the technology rears ahead of anything else. For example, one of my colleagues whom I see as a master teacher, especially when it comes to bringing together content, instructional goals, students' multiple literacies, and innovative, authentic practice, hit a wall during a recent lesson. Elizabeth was working with students to create digital narratives from footage they'd captured using small, USB video cameras. She'd planned this work out to what she described as a "micro-level," supporting students with graphic organizers, detailed descriptions, and an extensive rubric. She'd even tried out the project herself, explaining, "I did it myself on a student computer from the laptop cart. The goal was to troubleshoot so there weren't any surprises in a room of thirty." Despite that, first period was a jumble of confusion as the laptops didn't consistently "see" or recognize the video cameras as students worked to move their footage, files that did move wouldn't open, and no two computers were acting the same.

When we debriefed, she'd had two days to reflect on the activity, her initial response, the shifts she made throughout the day, and the ways that students were able to reach their end goal. Looking across her approach, three qualities or steps emerged that are useful in thinking about what to do when the technology "hiccups" or prevents us from moving student learning, reading and/or writing in the ways we'd originally designed. Bottom line—at some point in time in your teaching, this will happen—no matter how tightly planned or experienced you are. It won't happen each time, but knowing what to do when it does matters.

She explained her first reaction during first period as a mix of frustration and disbelief, "I'd prepped so tightly and had such a narrow window of time that I utterly had to fight back the urge to completely retreat." Students were completing this project at the close of their unit—and two days before the end of the grading period. Critical to her success in moving forward were two ideas, neither of which was unique to teaching with technology. She offered, "Any time that I do something with my students, it has the potential to hit some bumps. The key is to be as patient as I can in the thick of it, and to bring in any expertise I can find." In some cases,

Strategies for When the Technology Fails:

1. Do as much upfront planning as possible (including trying the assignment yourself on students' computers.)

2. Exhibit patience under fire.

3. Model your questioning for students while troubleshooting or rethinking the assignment.

4. Look to students as experts.

5. Leverage the expertise in your building.

6. Frontload your teaching with content and learning goals rather than "technology"-driven practices to ensure a "plan B."

Elizabeth will draw on the knowledge of her reading specialist or literacy coach in the building. In others, she reaches out to the technology specialist or colleagues (in the building or within her online network) who have done similar work in past terms.

If there is a best practice in managing those moments where the technology doesn't do what we expected, it is usually to model our thinking and questioning process for students. As discussed throughout the book, students need our model as sophisticated readers and writers, but they also need to see how we work with new and emerging tools to do the work that is central to our discipline. They need us to model flexibility. They need to see us "think aloud" our process in moving from a task/use that isn't working to one that does. Doing so as authentically and honestly as possible is as much a part of co-constructing literacy practices alongside students as it is work that helps to further establish the learning community in the classroom. It makes it "okay" for students to wrestle alongside us.

Learning to Leverage and Build Resources: Reaching Outward

Engaging students in new literacies practices with digital media requires not only creativity and ingenuity on your part as teacher but a support structure that helps to move you through the work. There are teaching contexts rich with these kinds of supports: resource-rich classrooms or departments, openings in the curriculum for teacher and student creativity, instructionally minded technology support staff, encouraging parents, policies for bringing new tools and websites into classroom use, and/or forward-thinking administrators who trust our expertise. Across my work in multiple states, I have yet to see a context where all of these are in place. In some instances, we luck out by finding three or more of these supports, and, in the majority, we are lucky to find one or two.

No matter how great your motivation to engage students in this work, context does matter. And, in unlocking sites or securing resources, there are ways to advocate for support that will advance your work. As discussed earlier in this book, none of these recommendations are "silver bullets," which when yielded will result in resources and support raining down upon your classroom. However, they are strategies that call attention to students' successes, students' needs, and those openings and opportunities that would help to move your work to a more supported, richer place.

Strategies for Securing Support:

1. Enacting an open-door policy.

2. Engaging parents through transparency and safety.

3. Establishing symposiums/galleries of student work.

4. Getting students' work out into the community.

5. Sharing research and practitioner articles with colleagues and administrators.

6. Presenting your work at conferences.

We wrestle against two looming realities when it comes to teaching with digital media: assessment and filtering. We've discussed assessment in each of the strategy chapters of this book in examining how teachers authentically assess multimodal or new literacies work in a culture which often puts the metrics measured by standardized assessments at the forefront of curriculum. As important as it is to think about your pedagogy and instruction in dialogue with the assessments that students are held accountable for passing, it is critical to also consider the ways in which new media and collaborative texts require a different rubric and set of criteria than captured in most curricula. In developing those tools, I typically work alongside teachers in my university department who bring their expertise in teaching ninth-grade or twelfth-grade curricula. Together, we work to gather our insights on the curriculum, what students need to know and be able to do, and the unique affordances of multimodal or new media-rich assignments.

The biggest obstacle that I face when working with teachers in the field, teaching in my own classroom, or offering a professional development workshop is the filter in place in any given school or district. While I am the first to acknowledge that there is copious objectionable material available online that I don't want appearing in my classroom, there are useful tools and resources to be accessed that I regularly can't get to through the filter and/or firewall. Filtering complicates what is already challenging work in our classrooms, and, further, it requires a different level of advocacy on our part in the instances where we need to "open" a site blocked through a school filter.

It often surprises teachers that, in most cases, something *can* be done to allow students to gain access to a site or resource. In my practice, advocating to technology support folks and administrators can make a difference. But, in doing so, we need to speak their language. We need to explain the educational impact of a site (which they likely don't know apart from considering it through the lens we provide through our discipline), and we need to talk about how students will use the site or resource within our teaching. While part of me always wants to use these dialogues to advocate for the broader harms that filters create, pulling back and focusing on one site at a time given the specific context of your instructional goals will have more impact.

What that suggestion doesn't assume is that you're working with/for an administrator who shares your pedagogical (and digital?) values. If step one of this process involves sharing instructional goals within your request to have a site "unblocked," step two needs to involve opening up your classroom to their participation. Invite your administrators to come into your classroom and see what you and your students will do with the site or resource. If you meet with resistance, offer that this work be done in a single class period, allowing for comparison of skills, learning, and development across sections that engage in a technology-infused approach against those that don't, keeping in mind that no class can be cleanly matched to another. The goal here isn't to create more work, but to invite your administrator or other colleagues to learn alongside you and your students. Doing so provides a proof of concept of not only what students accomplish but also what can happen when teachers work together as a learning community to explore potential pedagogies and resources.

Elizabeth took this thinking further, sharing her "findings" and student work through local and state professional conferences and in a K–12 online conference. She explained, "My principal was over the moon that kids were sharing their work within an audience of other teachers. He liked that they had something to say, and that their voices were valued by more than me." She also works with students at the end of each semester to generate a "wish list," noting the websites they need to access, hardware and software that would help in making their work more rigorous and relevant, and the learning goals that they had for their own new literacies practices. Copies of this list are posted in the classroom and are shared with the library/media specialist, technology support staff, English department chair, administration, and anyone else in a position to help move their thinking and resource pool further.

As important as attaining buy-in and support from your administration is, building those same attributes in the parents of your students is a vital component for making this work successful. Many parents respond well to our efforts to use technology to keep them in closer connection with class assignments (e.g., posting homework assignments to a class website), but grow concerned when the use of new literacies practices with digital media causes the classroom to look "too different" from what their experiences had been as students (e.g., using geotagged audio files to support work with students' place narratives). I've found that the best way to engage parents is similar to what I advocate for securing administrative support—be transparent about what you're doing, and, where possible, invite them into your classroom.

For example, Elizabeth maintains a class website that offers lists of homework assignments, access to student grades, and recommended resources. One page on the site (which she also duplicates and sends home in paper form to support families who lack Internet access at home) offers a class newsletter, sharing ideas about the units, readings, and activities to be explored. When class projects require technology or digital media, she offers descriptions of what parents can expect to see; a quick, brief rationale of the ways in which new literacies practices or digital media will enhance students' learning opportunities; and suggestions for how parents can talk with students about their work. She explained, "I'm both being public about my practice and saying to parents that it is okay that they don't know what this looks like in an English class. I'm on top of it, and that they can have a role if they want it. Few ever go that far, maybe because I invite them in the first place." Elizabeth emphasized that her work in being transparent about her teaching when engaging in more traditional activities as well as when working on new literacies situated work helped to further establish buy-in, "so I'm not catching anyone off guard by suddenly talking about what we are doing. Instead, we always have that conversation, and the door is always open."

Learning Alongside Our Students

The most important resource you have in supporting and developing your learning with digital media and new literacies practices is your students. Watch what they do. Ask hard questions, not only about where to point and click but also about what draws them to that space, how they engage with participatory media, what role their participation takes, and, most important, the ways that they learn to read and write outside of our classrooms.

This learning process started for me more than ten years ago when I sat down next to Elliott, a digitally literate eighth grader, and began to build my first teacher website. And, it continues to today as I plan to work with a group of tenth graders who are trying desperately to show me how Second Life can work as a learning space. My learning cannot stop as I want to be sure that while valuing literary analysis and language skills, I'm also helping students to access new literacy practices that are foundational to engaging in an uncertain future. And I need to make sure that these aren't experiences that are limited to the students in my classes who are independent learners or who, for a variety of reasons, don't yet engage in a "wired" world outside of the classroom. The key is to see, to listen, to value, and to learn. Together.

Glossary

Note: The challenge in writing a list like this is that the terms will likely shift some as the tools continue to develop. You might also look for more to be included here as new tools and capacities exist beyond the date this book went to press. The definitions here are meant to be just enough to help you engage with the writing in this book. For more, you'll have to go online, dig in, and play. . . .

Bebo: A popular social networking website where users create profiles and are able to comment on one another's pages, photo collections, etc. The students I work with use Bebo as a place for discovering new musicians' work through artists' profiles, though several do the same with MySpace.

Cloud computing: Software, storage, and resources made available online through an account login. (e.g., what once was stored or run from a computer can now be held and run online.)

Creative Commons Licenses: These licenses help to signal how content can be used, ranging from requiring attribution to the original writer/creator, to requirements about its use for commercial or share-alike purposes. Orienting students to how these licenses function is key to teaching them to understand how to use content they find online.

De.licio.us: A tool for social bookmarking. On the simplest level, users can post their bookmarks under a username/login so they can be accessed from any computer at any time. To aid in organization, bookmarks can be tagged. Users have the option to keep content private, to share it with specific users, or to make their bookmarks and tags public. The social part of the tool comes into play when it comes to sharing bookmarks or researching through tags or tag clusters.

Fanfiction sites: Websites where "fans" of particular works, characters, or settings/contexts share their own original writing using those same characters, places, plotlines, etc. Most sites allow for ratings to be posted, ranking and providing feedback to writers from other fans in the community.

Flickr: This is another website/sharing tool that can be used in a simple way or that can be used to engage in a participatory community. As such, Flickr can be used as a website for posting images that are then either private or publicly shared. I first used Flickr as a fast tool for sharing photos of my children with family. Other "layers" of the tool emerge with tagging, communities of users who come together as "groups," searching, and permissions following creative commons guidelines.

Gmail: A free email account with significant amounts of storage available to users who sign up for a free account with Google. This was one of the first "tools" developed by Google, leading users to see the company as about more than just a search engine.

Google Documents: A free, web-based, cloud-computing set of word processing, spreadsheet, presentation, and form tools made available through a Google account. Documents can be shared and edited by multiple users at the same time and require only a browser and Internet connection.

Mash-Up: A digital media file that brings together an assortment of text, images, audio, and motion/video files to create a new text.

Microblogging: A form of blogging in which writers are limited to 140 characters. Topics tend to be focused on single ideas, "status updates," or condensed URLs. Example tools include Twitter and Plurk.

Moodle: An open-source course management tool including spaces for teachers to post assignments, run assessments, create and foster collaborative discussions, etc. (Similar to Blackboard but free and continually developed by the community of user-programmers working on the open-source code that supports the tool.)

Ning: An online platform for building your own social network community. Important Ning communities for secondary English teachers include but are not limited to the NCTE Ning, the English Companion Ning, and the Classroom 2.0 Ning.

Podcast: Audio or video files available for free download. Listeners are able to subscribe to the podcast (i.e., allowing for automatic downloads when new content is made available) through a "podcatching" tool (i.e., iTunes) using RSS to locate new content.

RSS: (Real Simple Syndication). A "feed" (e.g., signal) communicating to an aggregator or feed reader that new material is on a site for listening/download.

Social networking tools: Websites (i.e., Facebook, MySpace, Bebo, Ning) for building groups or communities of people who have shared interests and reasons to come together online.

Skype: Software that allows users to make phone calls over the Internet. Calls between computers are free and can support multiple users (i.e., conference calls) or video through a webcam.

Twitter: A popular microblogging tool limiting "posts" to 140 characters. Posting here is referred to as "tweeting."

VoiceThread: An online digital storytelling tool, allowing users to post and sequence images and narration. Viewers have the option of posting audio or print comments. Stories can be made private or public.

Weblog: A website typically used to share ideas, descriptions of events, and comments in chronological order. Further, this "posted" content is responded to by others through comments. Some blog entries involve video (vlog) or audio (podcast). Blogs can be searched through specific search engines like Technorati.com

Wiki: A readable/writeable website inviting readers to add to/change/revise content as an editor. Changes are trackable and mapped chronologically.

Wordle: A free web tool resulting in a word cloud—a visual image of words dominantly used in a text inserted in the text field. For example, I can scan a portion of Whitman's "Song of Myself," insert that text into the text field in Wordle, and generate a word cloud reflecting the content of the passage. The size of words included in the word cloud is determined by the number of occurrences within the text.

Annotated Bibliography

Books

Anstey, Michèle, and Bull, Geoff
**Teaching and Learning Multiliteracies:
Changing Times, Changing Literacies.**
Newark, DE: International Reading Association,
2006. Print.

As much as this book addresses multiliteracies and multimodal texts, it is firmly rooted in pedagogy. So, where so many books focus on technology or ways of composing through multiple media (especially digital media), this one focuses on teaching. Although it is a deeply conceptual book, it asks hard questions. Anstey and Bull provide a voice that I want in my head as I'm thinking about what it means to teach and engage with new literacy practices across multiple media and multiple technologies.

Kist, William
**New Literacies in Action: Teaching and
Learning in Multiple Media.**
New York: Teachers College Press, 2005. Print.

Kist writes about "pioneers" throughout the book, highlighting innovative teaching that integrates new media into the secondary English curriculum. This is a pre-Web 2.0 book, so the examples of innovative practice are compelling now because of the transparency of the cases of teacher practice (and student learning) and the ways in which teachers model putting learning goals ahead of specific tools. Written from Kist's researcher voice, he skillfully "interprets," sharing instances of teacher practice, teacher reflection, and calling our attention to questions and challenges that emerge any time that we work to develop and move our teaching in new directions.

Knobel, Michele, and Lankshear, Colin
A New Literacies Sampler.
New Literacies and Digital Epistemologies, v. 29.
New York: Peter Lang, 2007. Print.

This book does just what the title indicates, offering a "sampling" of compelling chapters exploring new literacies practices with digital media alongside discussion of how research in English education and literacy studies is working to push our understanding in new directions. The writers/scholars/researchers/teachers whose work appears in this volume make up the "superstars" in the field. Further, this book is situated so strongly in ideas about pedagogy and literacy that it will be a timely, seminal work—unlike so many books on technology that are dated before they hit the shelves.

Pahl, Kate, and Rowsell, Jennifer, eds.
**Travel Notes from the New Literacy Studies:
Instances of Practice.**
New Perspectives on Language and Education.
Clevedon, UK: Multilingual Matters, 2006. Print.

My reading in the area of new literacies and emerging technologies lives in two places: one, works that help me understand how our work as readers and writers in digital spaces is theorized and, two, works that help me look into the practice of my colleagues as they learn alongside their students. This book brings together both of these goals, collecting the voices of the key thinkers in the field of new literacies studies as they examine instances of classroom practice. I also find the organization of the book to be helpful in organizing my own thinking, moving from a focus on identity to the intersection between local and global literacy practices to ideas about text to multimodal practice in the classroom. In other words, we move from individual practice to work within a community, and from an exploration of digital texts to ideas about how texts work and live within our classrooms.

Palfrey, John G., and Gasser, Urs
Born Digital: Understanding the First Generation of Digital Natives.
New York: Basic Books/Perseus, 2008. Print.

While I have read several books over the past few years that address the ways in which adolescents learn and engage within a digital world, this is the first I've come across that is steeped in an analysis of how we can learn from their literacy practices. As I discussed in Chapters Two and Three, Palfrey and Gasser also offer a framework that helps in understanding what it means to be "Born Digital"—building from but offering new insights on a generation described as "Digital Natives." Not written specifically to teachers, the book is ripe with insights that directly inform how adolescents learn, engage, and look to teachers for support and learning.

Shirky, Clay
Here Comes Everybody: The Power of Organizing without Organizations.
New York: Penguin Press, 2008. Print.

This isn't an "education" book but rather a book offering critical ideas about what participatory media and social networking tools mean for society, for work, and for communities. The quick summary: Meaningful group action is easier given ways new technologies allow us to connect with one another, share content and media, and work together to do something meaningful. This is a book exploring social changes, not a book that provides a model of what to do on Monday morning. That said, this is a book that has stayed with me in ways that strategy rich books rarely do, as seen by the multiple sticky notes, highlighted annotations, and, sadly, tape now holding pages to the binding.

Tapscott, Don
Grown Up Digital: How the Net Generation Is Changing Your World.
New York: McGraw-Hill, 2009. Print.

Though Tapscott works from the digital native thinking that I wrestle against, his book makes a compelling case for the ways in which digital youth are engaging with digital media to do meaningful, important work. It is a data-rich read, and one that doesn't shy away from the argument that as skilled as youth might be in working with digital media, few understand how to craft and manage a digital identity while safeguarding private information. This book builds on his original 1997 work, *Growing Up Digital: The Rise of the Net Generation*—a book that helped to set me down the path of exploring what technology could mean in my own teaching.

Research Studies

Ito, Mizuko, Heather A. Horst, Matteo Bittanti, danah boyd, Becky Herr-Stephenson, Patricia G. Lange, C. J. Pascoe, and Laura Robinson
Living and Learning with New Media: Summary of Findings from the Digital Youth Project.
Cambridge, MA: MIT Press, 2009. Print.

This is a report of current research on youth practices with digital media. Generated from a three-year project by scholars at the University of Southern California and University of California, Berkeley, findings are drawn from a large-scale ethnographic study of more than 660 youth and adults aged 10 to 30. Findings emphasize a distinction between friend-based and interest-based engagement in new media spaces.

Lenhart, Amanda, Sousan Arafeh, Aaron Smith, and Alexandra Macgill
Writing, Technology, and Teens.
Pew Internet & American Life Project. Web. 20 Nov. 2008.

This report highlights findings of a survey of 700 youth aged 12 to 17 and their parents on their writing practices in and outside of the classroom. Findings hold that while 93 percent of teens say they are writing for pleasure, just more than half of those same writers think of their work in digital environments (including text messages, emails, blogging) as writing that "counts." Teens and parents surveyed emphasized the importance of writing for success outside of the classroom. Data includes recommendations for teachers and classroom teaching.

Palfrey, John, Dena Sacco, danah boyd, Laura DeBonis, and Internet Safety Technical Task Force. ***Enhancing Child Safety and Online Technologies.*** Cambridge, MA: Berkman Center, Harvard University, 2009. Print.

While I am regularly frustrated by the ever-tightening filters that keep Internet access in schools confined and restricted, I also recognize the need to keep kids safe. This report is thick with data describing what schools, social networking and content companies running websites, and legislators are doing to raise awareness, protect children, and work with law enforcement to keep kids safe when working online. I read (and reread) the report to better understand the decisions administrators and technical support staff in buildings are faced with making, and, perhaps more important, to formulate my own arguments and ideas for how to best protect and empower students. This is the most comprehensive report available and well-worth multiple readings.

Recommended Journals

Practitioner journals that regularly feature articles addressing new literacies practices with digital media:

Language Arts (National Council of Teachers of English)

Voices from the Middle (National Council of Teachers of English)

English Journal (National Council of Teachers of English)

Educational Leadership (Association for Superintendents and Curriculum Developers)

Learning and Leading with Technology (International Society for Technology in Education)

Research journals that frequently feature articles addressing teacher practice and student learning with new literacies practices:

Research in the Teaching of English (National Council of Teachers of English)

Reading Research Quarterly (International Reading Association)

Journal of Research on Technology in Education (International Society for Technology in Education)

Contemporary Issues in Technology and Teacher Education—English Education Section (Jointly produced by the Society for Technology and Teacher Education and the Conference on English Education)

International Journal of Learning and Media (MIT Press)

Works Cited

Aducci, Romina, Pim Bilderbeek, Holly Brown, Seana Dowling, Nora Freedman, John Gantz, Abner Germanow, Takashi Manabe, Alex Manfrediz, and Shalini Verma "The Hyperconnected: Here They Come! A Global Look at the Exploding 'Culture of Connectivity' and Its Impact on the Enterprise." IDC White Paper, 2008. Web. 10 Sept. 2008.

Anstey, Michèle, and Geoff Bull. *Teaching and Learning Multiliteracies: Changing Times, Changing Literacies*. Newark, DE: International Reading Association, 2006. Print.

Applebee, Arthur N. "What Should High School English Be?" In Don Zancanella, "Dripping with Literacy, a Jazz-Fueled Road Trip, a Place to Breathe." *English Journal* 97.2 (2007): 71–78. Print.

Bauerlein, Mark. *The Dumbest Generation: How the Digital Age Stupefies Young Americans and Jeopardizes Our Future (Or Don't Trust Anyone Under 30)*. New York: Jeremy P. Tarcher/Penguin, 2008. Print.

Biancarosa, Gina, and Catherine E. Snow. *Reading Next—A Vision for Action and Research in Middle and High School Literacy: A Report to Carnegie Corporation of New York*. Washington, DC: Alliance for Excellent Education, 2004. Print.

boyd, danah michele. *Taken Out of Context: American Teen Sociality in Networked Publics*. Diss. University of California, Berkeley, 2008. Print.

boyd, danah. "Why Youth (Heart) Social Network Sites: The Role of Networked Publics in Teenage Social Life." *MacArthur Foundation Series on Digital Learning—Youth, Identity, and Digital Media Volume*. Ed. David Buckingham. Cambridge: MIT Press, 2007. Print.

Bruner, Jerome S. *Actual Minds, Possible Worlds*. Cambridge: Harvard U P, 1986. Print.

Bryant, J. Alison, Ashley Sanders-Jackson, and Amber M. K. Smallwood. "IMing, Text Messaging, and Adolescent Social Networks." *Journal of Computer-Mediated Communication* 11.2 (2006): 577–592. Web. 3 Dec. 2008.

Burke, Jim. *The English Teacher's Companion: A Complete Guide to Classroom, Curriculum, and the Profession*. 2nd ed. Portsmouth, NH: Heinemann, 2003. Print.

Cope, B., and Kalantzis, M. "Multiliteracies: The Beginning of an Idea." *Multiliteracies: Literacy Learning and the Design of Social Futures*. Eds. B. Cope and M. Kalantzis. London: Routledge, 2000. Print.

Gee, James Paul. "Chapter 3: Identity As an Analytic Lens for Research in Education." *Review of Research in Education* 25.1 (2000): 99–125. Print.

Goldberg, Amie, Michael Russell, and Abigail Cook. (2003). "The Effect of Computers on Student Writing: A Meta-Analysis of Studies from 1992 to 2002." *Journal of Technology, Learning and Assessment* 2 (2003): 1–51. Print.

Hannon, Celia, Peter Bradwell, and Charles Tims. *Video Republic*. European Cultural Foundation Report. London: Demos, 2008. Web. 10 Oct. 2008.

Hansen, Jane. *When Writers Read*. Portsmouth, NH: Heinemann, 2001. Print.

Harris, Judith B. "TPCK in In-Service Education: Assisting Experienced Teachers' 'Planned Improvisations.'" *Handbook of Technological Pedagogical Content Knowledge (TPCK) for Educators*. Ed. American Association of Colleges for Teacher Education Committee on Innovation and Technology. New York: Routledge for the American Association of Colleges for Teacher Education, 2008. 251–271. Print.

Horrigan, John, and Lee Rainie. *The Internet's Growing Role in Life's Major Moments*. Pew Internet & American Life Project, 2006. Web. 3 Jan. 2008.

Hull, Glynda A., and Mark Evan Nelson. "Locating the Semiotic Power of Multimodality." *Written Communication* 22.2 (2005): 224–261. Print.

Ito, Mizuko, Heather A. Horst, Matteo Bittanti, danah boyd, Becky Herr-Stephenson, Patricia G. Lange, C. J. Pascoe, and Laura Robinson. *Living and Learning with New Media: Summary of Findings from the Digital Youth Project*. Cambridge: MIT Press, 2008. Print.

Jones, Sydney, and Susannah Fox. *Generations Online*. Pew Internet & American Life Project, 2009. Web. 10 Feb. 2009.

Kajder, Sara. "Reading Online." *Reading on the Edge: Enabling, Empowering, and Engaging Middle School Readers*. Eds. Leigh Van Horn and Kylene Beers. Norwood, MA: Christopher Gordon, 2009. Print.

———. *The Tech-Savvy English Classroom*. Portland, ME: Stenhouse, 2003. Print.

———. "Unleashing the Potential with Emerging Technologies." *Adolescent Literacy: Turning Promise into Practice*. Eds. Kylene Beers, Robert E. Probst, and Linda Rief. Portsmouth, NH: Heinemann, 2007. Print.

Kress, G., and Street, B. "Multimodality and Literacy Practices." Eds. K. Pahl and J. Rowsell. *Travel Notes from the New Literacy Studies*. Bristol: Multilingual Matters, 2006. Print.

Kress, Gunther. "Editorial." *English in Education* 40.1 (2006): 1–4. Print.

Lee, Jihyun, Wendy S. Grigg, and Patricia L. Donahue. *The Nation's Report Card: Reading 2007 (NCES 2007–496)*. Washington, DC: National Center for Education Statistics, Institute of Education Sciences, U.S. Department of Education, 2007. Print.

Lemke, Jay. "New Media and New Learning Communities." National Council of Teachers of English Assembly for Research, Feb. 2007, Nashville. Print.

Lenhart, Amanda, and Mary Madden. *Social Networking Sites and Teens: An Overview*. Pew Internet and American Life Project, 2007. Web. 2 June 2008.

Lenhart, Amanda, Mary Madden, Alexandra Macgill, and Aaron Smith. *Teens and Social Media*. Washington DC: Pew Internet & American Life Project, 2007. Web.11 Jan. 2009.

Lenhart, Amanda, Sousan Arafeh, Aaron Smith, and Alexandra Macgill. *Writing, Technology, and Teens*. Pew Internet & American Life Project, 2008. Web. 20 Nov. 2008.

Lenhart, Amanda, and Mary Madden. *Teens, Privacy, and Online Social Networks*. Pew Internet and American Life Project, 2007. Web. 1 Aug. 2008.

Lenhart, Amanda, Mary Madden, and Paul Hitlin. *Teens and Technology: Youth Are Learning the Transition to a Fully Wired and Mobile Nation*. Pew Internet & American Life Project, 2005. Web. 17 June 2008.

Lenhart, Amanda, and Mary Madden. *Teen Content Creators and Consumers*. Pew Internet & American Life Project, 2005. Web. 17 June 2008.

Leu, Donald. J., Rachel A. Karchmer, Marla H. Mallette, and Julia Kara-Soteriou. "Contextualizing the New Literacies of Information and Communication Technologies in Theory, Research, and Practice." *Innovative Approaches to Literacy Education*. Eds. Donald J. Leu, Rachel A. Karchmer, Marla H. Mallette, and Julia Kara-Soteriou. Newark, DE: International Reading Association, 2005. 1–11. Print.

Leu, Donald J., Charles K. Kinzer, Julie L. Coiro, and Dana W. Cammack. "Toward a Theory of New Literacies Emerging from the Internet and Other ICT." *Theoretical Models & Processes of Reading*. 5th ed. Eds. R. B. Ruddell and N. Unrau Newark, DE: International Reading Association, 2004. 1570–1613. Print.

Li, Charlene. (2008). *Youth and Social Networks*. From North American Social Technographics Online Survey, Q2 2007. Cambridge: Forrester Research. Print.

Macgill, Alexandra. *Teens and Social Media*. Pew Internet & American Life Project, 2007. Web. 17 June 2008.

Mahiri, Jabari. "Digital DJ-ing: Rhythms of Learning in an Urban School." *Language Arts* 84.1 (2006): 55–62. Print.

McIntosh, Ewan. "How to Help People Better Use the 'Net." edu.blogs.com, 2009. Web. 19 March 2009.

McGrail, Ewa. "It's a Double-Edged Sword, This Technology Business." *Teachers College Record* 108.6 (2006): 1055–1079. Print.

Moje, Elizabeth Birr, Josephine Peyton Young, John E. Readence, and David W. Moore. "Teenagers in New Times: A New Literacy Studies Perspective. *Journal of Adolescent & Adult Literacy* 43 (2000): 400–411. Print.

Moje, Elizabeth Birr, Melanie Overby, Nicole Tysvaer, and Karen Morris. "The Complex World of Adolescent Literacy: Myths, Motivations, and Mysteries." *Harvard Educational Review* 78.1 (2008): 107–154. Print.

Moll, Luis C., Cathy Amanti, Deborah Neff, and Norma Gonzalez. "Funds of Knowledge for Teaching: Using a Qualitative Approach to Connect Homes and Classrooms." *Theory into Practice* 31.2 (1992): 132–141. Print.

National Endowment for the Arts. *Reading on the Rise: A New Chapter in American Literacy*. Washington, DC: National Endowment for the Arts, 2009. Print.

New London Group. "A Pedagogy of Multiliteracies: Designing Social Futures." *Harvard Educational Review* 66.1 (1996): 60–92. Print.

O'Brien, David G. "Struggling Adolescents' Engagement in Multimediating: Countering the Institutional Construction of Incompetence." *Reconceptualizing the Literacies in Adolescents' Lives*. 2nd ed. Eds. Donna E. Alvermann, Kathleen A. Hinchman, David W. Moore, Stephen F. Phelps, and Diane R. Waff. Mahwah, NJ: Erlbaum, 2006. Print.

Palfrey, John "How Digital Natives Experience News." 2006. Web. 19 Oct. 2008.

Palfrey, John G., and Gasser, Urs. *Born Digital: Understanding the First Generation of Digital Natives*. New York: Basic Books/Perseus Books, 2008. Print.

Pew Internet Group. "Teens, Parents, and Technology: Highlights from the Pew Internet Project." 2003. Web. 26 March 2009.

Project Tomorrow. "Our Voices, Our Future: Student and Teacher Views on Science, Technology, and Education." National Report on Net Day's 2005 Speak Up Event, 2007. Web. 1 Nov. 2008.

Rheingold, Howard. "Using Participatory Media and Public Voice to Encourage Civic Engagement." *Civic Life Online: Learning How Digital Media Can Engage Youth*. Ed. W. Lance Bennett. The John D. and Catherine T. MacArthur Foundation Series on Digital Media and Learning, Cambridge: MIT Press, 2008. 97–118. Print.

Rideout, Victoria J., Donald F. Roberts, and Ulla Foehr. *Generation M: Media in the Lives of 8–18 Year-Olds*. Washington, DC: Henry J. Kaiser Family Foundation, 2005. Web. 17 June 2008.

Robnolt, Valerie, Joan Rhodes, and Judy Richardson. *Study Skills for the Twenty-First Century: Creating a New Model*. Miami: National Reading Conference, 2005. Print.

Shirky, Clay. *Here Comes Everybody: The Power of Organizing without Organizations*. New York: Penguin, 2008. Print.

Sundén, Jenny. *Material Virtualities: Approaching Online Textual Embodiment*. Digital Formations, v. 13. New York: Peter Lang, 2003. Print.

Tapscott, Don. *Grown Up Digital: How the Net Generation Is Changing Our World*. New York: McGraw-Hill, 2009. Print.

Thompson, Bob. "Unexpected Twist: Fiction Reading Is Up." *Washington Post* 12 Jan. 2009: C01. Print.

Weigel, Margaret, Carrie James, and Howard Gardner. "Learning: Peering Backward and Looking Forward in the Digital Era." *International Journal of Learning and Media* 1.1 (2009): 1–18. Print.

Wesch, Michael. "Participatory Media Literacy: Why It Matters." *Mediated Cultures*, 2009a. Web. 10 Jan. 2009.

Wesch, Michael. "A Vision of Students Today (and What Teachers Must Do)." *Britannica Blogs*, 2008. Web. 21 Oct. 2009.

Wesch, Michael. From Knowledgeable to Knowledge-Able: Learning in New Media Environments. *Academic Commons*, 2009b. Web. 27 Jan. 2009.

Wilber, Dana J. iLife: Understanding and Connecting to the Digital Literacies of Adolescents. *Best Practices in Adolescent Literacy Instruction*. Eds. Kathleen A. Hinchman and Heather K. Sheridan-Thomas. New York: Guilford, 2008. Print.

Index

Author

Sara Kajder is an assistant professor at Virginia Tech whose teaching has been anchored in assisting middle and high school students to connect out-of-school literacies with in-school literacies—including helping students create multimodal texts (such as blogs and digital stories), communicate their meaning-making through podcasts, and engage in Web 2.0 learning spaces, such as wikis, Twitter, and other tools. Regardless of the tool(s) we use, Kajder focuses on the uses of new literacies to affirm the literacies students bring into our classrooms, to produce knowledge, and to put students' knowledge to work. Recipient of the National Technology Leadership Fellowship, she is the author of *Bringing the Outside In* (2006) and *The Tech-Savvy English Classroom* (2003).

This book was typeset in Jansen Text and BotonBQ by
Barbara Frazier.

Typefaces used on the cover include American Typewriter,
Frutiger Bold, Formata Light, and Formata Bold.

The book was printed on 60-lb Williamsburg Recycled Offset
paper by Versa Press, Inc.

30% Total Recycled Fiber